This is the story of an ⁣ e
me). It's about addiction ⁣ e
mad, but giving way to l⁣ in forgiveness and faith. Gratitude that brought healing to life.

The power of finding and living the life of your soul. Learning to love, and trying to be kind without apology. To live free, to truly comprehend what it is like to live free, without judgment, without fear.

In writing this story, there were two bridges I needed to cross. The first being, how does a woman who spent the majority of her life keeping everything inside handle the exposure? The second being, who am I to write about me? In both cases the answer that propelled me forward was always the same. There is someone out there who needs inspiration right now. If this can be a light in someone's darkness, I must pass it on.

Not all, but some of the names in this book have been changed to protect the innocent. I had considered using an alias then realized if I am going to discuss facing fears, and not living in the bondage of society's opinion, then I must find the courage to do this as me.

My prime directive while writing this book, was to cause no hurt to others. The most important blessing I received, was from my father. "You must tell the truth, it is not what you say but how you say it. " I knew he would understand, as any man or woman who has had their life torn apart will tell you......This journey is about truth and healing and forgiveness.

I hope you enjoy this book as much as I enjoyed the ride.

Wendy

Acknowledgement

To Kreso Nuic, Elation Design Studios – Thank you, thank you, thank you! I am forever grateful for the gift of your design talents. You captured my heart and my book with your cover design. It is not about what you see, but how it makes you feel, and you did that for me with enthusiasm and talent.

To Deb Jamieson – I cannot begin to thank you enough for undertaking the overwhelming challenge of editing my book. The hours upon hours you must have spent wrestling with tenses and punctuation is mind boggling. My free spirit creates free writing that needs a disciplinarian. I am incapable of embracing structure to the extent that you wanted me to. I know there are many more changes you would like to make, please know you are a genius in what you were able to accomplish with this unfocused student.

To Ryan Browne, Rys Designs – Thank you and Shannon for giving up so much of your limited time to do a couple of crazy woman photo shoots. It was so nice to be bossed around by a strong and calming force.

To Jessica Guerrero – Your advice during the early stages of my manuscript was very much appreciated and helpful. The kindness, you, a person I have never met extended to me only strengthens my belief in the inherent goodness of humanity.

To Cathy Keeler – Coffee, gratitude, honesty and dimes. You taught me so little is required to turn a life around.

To Barry – Because I said I would put you in my book and I love Newfies. This is my toast to a hard working, life loving, crazy

Newfoundlander, lost in Scarborough.

To my sounding boards – Shauna Brown, Michele Bush, Heather Clarke, Marilyn Floyd, Laura Fowlie, Kim MacGregor, Karen Rae, Janet Rogers, Debbie Sidock, Susan Snell. Each one of you read parts of my book as it developed. Your input, your understanding and your encouragement meant so much to this woman who was trying to conquer fear and doubt.

To my BBG – May we never grow up, may we always laugh and may there always be bread for Donna.

To Jim Doucher and Cindy Fairbairn – April 23, 2014, was the night that changed my life. I am forever grateful for the two of you. We have shared in Elisa's journey for over a decade but on that night the two of you were a major part of the events that brought me gratitude.

To Elisa Linton – You have been my silent teacher for almost 20 years now. The lessons you have provided and the love you have shared. I do not think I have met anyone who has impacted more lives than you. Your legacy may very well end up being a cure for Sanfilippo Syndrome, but your most far reaching legacy will be the promise of hope inspired by the actions of faith.

To the employees at Wizbot – I am incredibly grateful. The words that are needed go beyond an acknowledgment page. One day soon we will have our cake!

To Dan – I still don't have the words … maybe they have not been invented.

To my family – You are my daily reminder that I am blessed and life is awesome.

—ₘ—

This book is dedicated to the memory of my mother.

Mom – your kindness, courage and grace
were second only to your capacity to love.

I am – forever grateful.

Sandra Hill (Rae), née MacPhee

May 30, 1939 – June 7, 2012

Cover Art: Kreso Nuic, **Elation Design Studios**

Cover Photography: Ryan Browne, **Rys Designs**

Typography: David Galway, **Wizbot Inc.**

Printed in Oakville, Ontario, Canada, by **Wizbot Inc.**

Table of Contents

Forward · i

Chapter 1 – **The Seed** · · · · · · · · · · · · · · · · · 1

Chapter 2 – **Building Blocks** · · · · · · · · · · · · ·15

Chapter 3 – **Prepare** · · · · · · · · · · · · · · · · ·29

Chapter 4 – **Fly Like An Eagle** · · · · · · · · · · ·55

Chapter 5 – **Mr. C** · · · · · · · · · · · · · · · · · ·73

Chapter 6 – **The Eagle Changes to The Wolf** · · · · ·87

Chapter 7 – **The Birth of Wizbot** · · · · · · · · · 101

Chapter 8 – **The Ides of March** · · · · · · · · · · 115

Chapter 9 – **Discovery** · · · · · · · · · · · · · · ·139

Chapter 10 – **Soulless** · · · · · · · · · · · · · · ·157

Chapter 11 – **The Intervention** · · · · · · · · · · 177

Chapter 12 – **Forgiveness** · · · · · · · · · · · · · 195

Chapter 13 – **The Truth** · · · · · · · · · · · · · · 211

Chapter 14 – **Sanctuary** · · · · · · · · · · · · · · 229

You Are Not The Boss Of Me

All of my life, I have said I would write a book one day. I have started to, I have wanted to. At times I thought I needed to, but before now, I have never been able to. This time is different, I am not writing because I want to be a writer, and I am not writing because I have some great idea for the perfect story. Today I have started writing because it is time, I am ready. The story is in me. It is a lifetime in the making, every step, every turn and every lesson learned. It has been a journey full of highs and lows, but mostly highs, that is until I found the lowest of lows. No median for me, no coasting on a smooth path at a comfortable speed, just one big amazing adventure.

This book was born out of my journey through depression and my final decision to leave my partner of 24 years. My walk through the shame of hurting someone I had loved weighed against the pain of staying in misery. Trying to live with a decision I had to make that went against everything I thought I knew about myself.

Stubborn. Naïve. Foolish. A head full of romantic sentiments. "You Are Not the Boss of Me" should be tattooed on my forehead, as while desperate to prove I was worthy, I was so filled with an overwhelming desire to be free. Freedom, the most basic of human needs: free to love, free to hate, free to run or to stay, but free nonetheless to live the life you were born to.

Love yourself and always, always be yourself. As long as you are true to you, then you will find yourself surrounded by great friends who love you for who you are, not who you pretend to be. How empty would it be, to fill your life with people who are attracted to your mask, as opposed to the real you? How stressful to have to bite your tongue or hide your heart, so as not to let on that everything is make believe! If you live the life of you, then it will be filled with hearts and souls that keep you whole. They will love you for who you are as they will know and understand your shortcomings. They will accept your imperfections and embrace all these things as part and parcel of being with you.

I love interacting with people, most of the time, except when I need air, wide open space, and an escape from suffocation. I feel connections, sense fear and share pain. Life to me is a raw nerve. Living so exposed can lead to euphoria or depression. I don't walk in a room and see the decor, I can never describe much of what I just saw, but I feel it. I feel the mood of the people. Does everybody? This I do not know.

I am scattering thoughts on this page. The empty space on the screen overwhelms me. The story in my head becomes less inviting when it moves down to my fingers and onto the keyboard. I have come to recognize that writing this will leave me bare, that if my life really is the search for truth, then I must accept that the truth is not always pleasant, but it will set me free. So as you read this, know that there are moments where I am lying naked in the street. Vulnerable and exposed, open to ridicule and scathing judgements. Yet I will do this, for I know what it is like to hit rock bottom and once you have lost everything, there is nothing life can take from you that hurts anymore. You are now free. Free to embrace life, to dance and to love stronger, more intensely, more passionately, without restrictions, without chains.

I can forgive myself the consequences of imperfect actions made without knowledge. It is the actions of intent that keep me awake. I do not want what is not mine, not the extra $10 the cashier accidentally gives me or the camera left behind in error. These things I did not earn and are not there for my taking. At the same time should I fail to notice the additional change or should I grab an item thinking it was mine by accident, then I harbour no guilt. My life has been filled with moments where I have been tested. Sometimes I passed and sometimes I failed miserably. I accept that no one is perfect. I strive to do better, most of the time, but not always. I am human and so it is here that I begin my story, the journey of a simple woman who set out to build a life on a wing and a prayer, freedom and faith:

You Are Not The Boss Of Me.

Chapter 1

The Seed

This seed you are planting shall grow.
Choose wisely in your approach.

Will there be storms to weather?
Will there be enough sunlight, enough warmth?
Will there be enough water?

Choose wisely in your approach.

Will it have enough nourishment in its youth,
to grow strong and be healthy for years to come?
Will it have enough love to continuously bear fruit, and be
secure no matter how harsh the winter comes?

This seed that is planted shall grow.
Choose wisely in your approach.

It has been five months now, five months and over 1000 kilometres walked and 32 pounds lost. I had set out to find myself again. I had started walking for answers, holding onto the feeling of joy I had tasted – ever so aware of the breath of life I had taken. I am in a time of change, although I say I am finding myself again, I am very much aware of the new self that has entered my life. There is a vanity that never existed before, a need to fix every part of myself. It does not consume me, but it intrigues me. Part of who I am / was has always been a lack of exterior self interest. I wanted to discover life from the inside; what is in me and what can I achieve from there.

The new me is different, I have awoken to a whole new world. That which defined me when I was young is no longer relevant. I have nothing to prove. Ego dissipates with age or is it experience?

So I look in the mirror and I see the physical me: the swelling has gone, the grey removed, the fat is being toned and the size 12/14 is now a 4/6. Nothing old fits. I have to start a new wardrobe – just like my life. I am a little lost and confused. I don't know how to dress. I am feeling so young, so alive and so full of adventure. My heart feels 27, but I am 51. Like someone with a near death experience, this is my second chance at life.

This body has a shape now. Did I ever have a shape? Did I ever care? I am sure I did, but it was never as important as being strong and independent. I wanted to walk strong, to show I was invincible – or something. Not now. Now at the age of 51, I want to be a woman. It is awkward. It is hard to comprehend. I don't know how to walk this walk, but I want to. I am alive in ways I never felt before, or at least I am no longer ashamed to feel these things.

My heart is also frightened, anxious. It is awake, vulnerable and terribly afraid that time will run out before it finds its home: not any home, but its home. There is a difference. Afraid it may not find a home, afraid to go through this life without ever finding a soulmate. I had yearned to be free and yet now I worry about being alone. I contradict myself. I am not alone in this. I find solace in the fact I am in a much better place today than I have known in forever. I know I will resolve this contradiction, my logical side tells me to embrace the freedom and heal myself. There is so much healing to do. I am where I am meant to be right now. Those 10 words bring me comfort, they take the past and the future out of the equation. From this moment in time I go forward. I inhale this breath of life. I let it fill my lungs, my heart and my soul. I exhale. I taste it. I savour it. I am exactly where I am meant to be right now.

As I wake up, as I find myself recovering, reinventing myself, a new me. So different in some ways, the same in others. I have a clarity that did not exist before, an understanding of life, of me, of happiness. I was an island for the vast majority of my life. I liked it. I embraced it and I believed it. I have come to terms with my issues with relationships. As an island there was no room for receiving, and not enough of a base for truly giving of myself – truly giving myself. Those words fill me with passion. I envision another plateau, something beautiful I have yet to experience.

Me, the person, the island, understood life to be about self control, to be about duty and responsibility. Weakness was to be avoided. Although I could see where I was failing in self control, they were minor abuses. All that was required to overcome them was more strength and less weakness, more self restraint. The harder things got the more I turned inward. People trying to help became burdens. I felt they were adding to my misery. I could not pay them back so I was trying to escape friends and family. I wanted those obligations to stop piling up. Every kind deed became another thing owed. I had nothing to give in return. I was empty.

Now however, as I write this book, as I take inventory and go through this journey of self discovery, my understanding of how love and happiness fit, of where they fit, has grown exponentially. Life is not a duty; it is a gift. I have a duty to respect life, to honour life, to nurture life, but living in and of itself is not a duty. I knew that at one time. I knew that more than most. I used to believe I was one of the happiest people on the planet, even when I could hardly make ends meet. I had so much peace and happiness in my heart. How did I ever manage to lose sight of the joy in living? It was not that I had nothing left to give, but that I was no longer grateful. When my rose coloured glasses fell off, I let anger and doubt fill my soul. I could no longer see beauty and joy. Without those glasses, I let gratitude slip away.

My father is an outgoing, friendly crazy character, full of life, love and energy. He always wants to make people feel at ease and happy. He's never afraid to speak to a stranger and always quick with a joke, corny or otherwise. He loves to make people laugh. It is his way of giving. Dad is an expert in making people feel comfortable at his own expense. He does not care if he looks foolish; he just cares that they feel good. I think happy people understand that position. We may look like idiots, but we are controlling our environment by filling our surroundings with good things.

When we were children growing up on the outskirts of Montreal, Dad would build a skating rink in our back yard every winter. I spent so much time lying on, crawling on, skating on the ice – it was my happy place. I loved the speed. I always wanted to push my legs harder. How much faster could I go? How quick could I stop? How sharp could I turn? I spent hours on that rink. On those freezing cold crisp winter nights, bundled in a snow suit, I remember staring at the stars, feeling intensely at peace. The open air and the vast universe filled me with a feeling I could never put into words. It was humbling, beckoning, reassuring. I was in harmony with it.

My Dad was always building, fixing or tinkering. He was a doer, always doing something and seeming to have fun no matter what it was. I wish I could say I remember he and my mother being in love, but that is not the case. It's more like I remember them arguing and me trying to find a place to run away to. I could not stand to be in the house if it was not happy.

My brother's friends would call Dad "The Fonz". He was so cool and funny, especially when he was drinking. As a young child, I did not understand the implications of Dad's drinking, just that it made Mom upset. Since he seemed so happy, I sometimes thought she was ruining the fun. As I got older, I started to understand. I did not like the time Dad was drunk while refereeing my ringette game. It hurt to hear people yelling for the drunk to get off the ice. That was my father. People were so cruel. I loved my Dad and I thought he was the coolest most awesome man on the planet. He is a pretty awesome man, however like his father before him, Dad was an alcoholic.

Fortunately, unlike his father, my Dad found his sobriety around the age of 38. Like many alcoholics, he had to hit rock bottom. He lost everything: the house, his car, his job and most of all his family. As if his life was not bad enough, living in a small, nasty little room in Montreal, Dad was mugged and every penny he owned was gone. It would have had to have been a moment where anyone would have questioned their will to go on, but go forward Dad did, this time leaving the bottle behind him forever.

I am proud of my father. I feel no anger for his alcoholism. I went to enough AA meetings with him when I was a child, to understand his battle. There were wonderful people at those meetings: important people, rich people, mothers, people from so many different backgrounds with equally sad and compelling stories. Quite often, at least from my vantage point, they had some of the best senses of humour and the most amazing outlooks on life. A room full of ex drunks telling stories of their not so glorious days. You knew that most of them knew how to be the life of the party, and now here they were partying on coffee, laughing and living right out loud. Life did not end for them at the bottom. It began anew.

I am very much a product of my father. I will play the fool for a laugh. I love seeing joy and watching people smile. Even in the simple things like grocery shopping. I love it, I love the interaction with people and the knowledge I might bump into someone I have not seen for a while. I can get so high that sometimes I am flying. I see the world as a field of opportunity and adventure. I don't want to land, 10 feet off the ground is a great way to live. My heart some days is bursting with gratitude and love. I cannot explain how good it feels to live so free, to find joy in the little things, to not need the big expensive things. My Dad gave me that, this powerful sense that every day is a gift just waiting to be opened. I know the lows as well. Not that much bothers or hurts me. I don't worry much what others say or think, but as I recently discovered, to have my wings clipped, to be grounded and not able to fly, that took the life right out of me.

Also like my father, I have an addictive personality. Smoking, drinking, gambling. Thankfully for me it only took two trips to Vegas to realize I will never play black jack again. The smoking, well that is my next challenge. I call it my best friend and my worst enemy. For someone so obsessed with freedom, it's amazing how long I have let tobacco control me. I often think I smoke because I am so desperately missing something more important in my life. That may be true, for it is not just the nicotine addiction. It is the solace I find in the action of running away, just my cigarette and me. Almost like I believe an answer is to be found every time I inhale. Together we will conquer, we will be victorious, we will find the truth.

But alcohol, my dear sweet drink, my stupid juice, my energizer. What I thought to be my best writing friend, or my liquid courage. It will be two years next month since I gave up the bottle. Red wine was my favourite thing in the world. Someone once said to me, "How can you be an alcoholic? You never did anything bad because of it." Well that is just it, isn't it? After all I have lived, and all I know about alcoholism, allowing it to be the catalyst of a negative life changing moment would kill me. Hitting rock bottom because of alcohol abuse was the one thing I would never be able to forgive myself for. And yet I did. I did hit rock bottom, it just wasn't so obvious at the time… And I do forgive myself. It has not been easy, but life went on and I am a better person today because of it.

It was four months after my mother passed that I finally found the power to quit drinking. My self loathing over her death was the impetus, if I was not miserable enough, I was going to make myself more miserable. My life had become impossible to manage. I found myself crying every day. The loss in and of itself was overwhelming, but it was also how I felt I failed her that was eating away at me. Between my daughter Jodie needing her mother, and my needing clarity and salvation, I somehow found the strength to stop drinking.

I used to be ashamed of it, not anymore. Like someone with a peanut allergy, who loves peanut butter but knows it could kill them, I knew what wine was doing to me. I loved it, but it was killing me. I could feel it passing through my veins. I could see the swelling in my face, and feel the pain in my stomach. Worst of all though, was the obsession, the control it had over me. It is not the third drink that kills you, for me it was the first. After that who knew when I would have enough.

How do I do it? How do I say I will never drink again? I don't. I don't know the answer. I just know that today I am not drinking, and that today I am happier and in a better place. I know I don't want to go through the process of quitting again. It was one of the hardest and greatest things I ever did. I know I want to be sober for Jodie. I know that this clarity of vision, this feeling of control is better then any high I ever got from alcohol. I love to party. I will always love to party and be with my friends. I love the silliness and the freedom that juiced-up laughter brings. It took time, I would say over a year without drinking for my emotions, needs and feelings to become clearer, and for my body to heal. Never in my life have I been filled with so much passion. There are no words to explain the joy, the ache, the inner peace and the inexplicable desires. I feel like I have been filled with some secret meaning of life. Everything I want, desire, need or can dream is obtainable without money, without possession. With this breath of life I was given, I have all I need to find my way. I have control and hope again. I have an adventure ahead of me, inspired by the simpleness of being. Had I not quit drinking, I doubt the intervention that changed my life would have happened.

It was winter, or maybe early spring, I was 13 and asleep in my own room. It was so nice to finally have my own room. We had a nice house now, a side split, and had lived in the same place for a couple of years. My Dad finished this room in the basement for me, and he even made the closet door handle out of wood carved with my initials. Defining moments live with us forever. The feelings, the fear, the pain – those things subside so we can live on, but those moments set the wheels in motion as to how we conduct our lives, they help form our view of the world.

I woke up to my mother screaming for help. I think it was 4:18 am. I could be wrong but whatever time it was that moment burned in my mind for years. I ran up the stairs from the basement screaming "Mom". My nine year old sister Cherin was having a sleep over. The kids were screaming. My brother was at the front door yelling "Mom, it's okay, he's gone!" I got to the door and saw my mother banging on the neighbour's door in her nightgown screaming, "Help me!" I saw a man running down the street. I yelled "Dad" and was about to run after him, but my brother held me back. I was scared and confused. What was going on? Why was my mother crying? I remember going upstairs and seeing blood on the wall, my Dad asleep on the couch. I was confused. If he was there, then who was running down the street? My mother, now back in the house held me, we just cried and held each other. The police arrived. I don't remember how soon, or how they entered. I must have been ushered to the basement for the rest I gathered from overhearing. I heard the police trying to awaken my father. My sisters friends … I don't know if they were picked up or driven home by the police. I was in my room, frightened and crying. To see my mother in distress was scaring me, hurting me, I don't think the police officer on the downstairs phone knew I was there, he was talking about a rape. I was not sure what the word meant, but I know what I thought it meant, and anger, hate, fear and disgust swept over me. I heard my Dad swearing, he must have woken up. He was throwing his briefcase against the wall. He was in so much pain, I loved my Dad so much. I was hurting for him. I was lost and confused, and could not put all the pieces together.

Eventually, through limited conversations with my brother, some answers came to me. My father had been drinking and brought a stranger home. When my Dad passed out the stranger had gone to the kitchen and started rustling through the drawers for a knife. My Mom awakened and went to the kitchen. The man forced her back to her room at knife point. My brother Greg, who was 15 almost 16 at the time, heard some noise and grabbed a chair. He confronted the man and chased him away. That is all I know. It was the night we were never allowed to speak of. Life went on. Mom and Dad divorced, we had to leave the house. We moved again and I dealt with the issues over time, but not without some emotional baggage. How could the incident not define my impression of being a woman, of sex and of feeling safe.

I spent the next several years hunting down that rapist in my mind. And each time I caught him, wondering if I would show him mercy, or if I would rid the world of him so he never hurt my Mom or anyone else again. I also perfected a tough girl walk, my outer shell. No one was going to mess with me. I was strong, to the point of feeling invincible. I developed a sixth sense. I was sure I would know danger and armed with just that sense, I walked through back alleys and walked alone, trying to break free of the fear hanging over me. For what seemed like years, I woke up every night at 4:18 am. In the beginning I was terrified and could not get back to sleep. As time went on I awoke just long enough to glimpse at the clock, an acknowledgement that I was winning. The fear, although not gone, was no longer in complete control of me.

I remember a few years later, a teacher in Grade 10 or 11, lecturing us on how it was never right to use violence, to hurt another human or to kill someone. She hit a nerve with me. I argued with her in class of how she would not know unless she walked in someone else's shoes, and that under certain circumstances we are all capable of such things. I shocked her and upset her. But I would not back down. In my head, there was a man with a knife; there were children in that house; he had an intent; it was not an accident; not a mistake; it was an intent to do harm. She would never know what I was thinking when I refused to back down. That moment, that class and that poor teacher, they were my therapy. I got it out the only way I could. I didn't tell the story, but I bulldozed her with my pent-up anger, I knew the difference between protecting the innocent and being evil; between self defence and intent to injure for personal gain. I knew what I had at one time believed I was capable of, what I believe every human being is capable of, they just need the right circumstances.

Finally it went from being an event that controlled me to one that shaped me, there was a lesson in it all, a message, an awareness. It has helped me feel compassion for others, bad things do happen to good people and good people like my Dad can do bad things, not on purpose, but by mistake. I wish people could understand the difference between intent and mistakes, I wish they would not be so quick to prosecute people for stupid mistakes but quicker to deal with bad intentions.

In all the years until her death, my mother and I never discussed that night. She was an amazing woman, a tiny woman with incredible internal fortitude. My respect and love for her grew stronger with the years as I became ever more aware of what she had given us; and what she had sacrificed.

—ᘏᘏ—

Although there was a lot to be learned in watching my father hit rock bottom, the real lesson was in seeing him get back up. He really did have nowhere to go but up, either that or give up, something a man like my father could never do.

Bankrupt and penniless, Dad found a job managing a "Pop Shoppe." The pay was dismal, but it was an opportunity. Living in the poorest of conditions, he somehow managed to squirrel away enough money to buy a used printing press for $100, not enough to buy a working one, but an abandoned one left in pieces. Dad had been a pressman for various companies when we were growing up. Although at this stage in his life I am sure running a press is the last thing he wanted to do, it was also his opportunity to dig himself out. So at night, after many hours of running the store all day, he started rebuilding that press. Over time he managed to get it working, then one cold call at a time, he started trying to build a printing business in the back of the shop at night.

Unable to get credit and with no one to turn to, he ploughed ahead. Slowly, but surely he built his dream. Eventually he outgrew that Pop Shoppe and opened Rae's Printing. It was not easy. There were many obstacles and I am sure many times he thought he might not make it. Yet he believed in himself and put in the time. He also remained sober. My Dad had cleaned up his act, as he liked to tell me.

Eventually the politics of running a business in Quebec got the best of Dad. The language laws and taxes ate away at him. He had met a nice woman. They married and moved back to the area of Dad's roots in Northern Ontario. He opened a small print shop and made an honest buck working hard and needing little. He did get married again, sold the shop and retired at 65. Today he is 75 and over 37 years sober. He is still cracking jokes, enjoying life with all his senses intact and, as he will tell you, he is in great shape for an old guy.

I am ever so aware that life is not full without the scars and the sadness. Everybody hurts. Everybody has their own journey filled with obstacles uniquely theirs. Life is about growing, about building, about overcoming, about being victorious over our fears. We require the darkness to appreciate the light. We need sorrow to truly feel joy. It is the combination of all things both good and bad unto ourselves and amongst our friends and family that drive us, inspire us and make us stronger, better, more caring and understanding.

To count our blessings, how could I forget that? Gratitude, whole hearted honest appreciation for this gift that is life.

Chapter 2

Building Blocks

To be fair or to be kind?
In kindness we teach love.
In fairness we teach entitlement.
It's not that fair is not kind,
But perhaps best held as an internal choice
Rather than an external expectation.

My sister Cherin is my inspiration. She gives, she fills cups everywhere she goes. If angels do exist, she is the angel of gratitude and giving. She has known that she has held the answers to my prayers all along, and tried in every way to bring me out of my depression. For weeks on end she sent me notes of inspiration and gratitude, taking the time to write and mail them. Every day, she tried everything in her power to lift me up and help me to see, however as the saying goes, there are none so blind as those who refuse to see.

It was not that I did not appreciate her notes. It is not that I did not read them. It was not that I was not grateful for the effort. I was extremely grateful. It was just that I thought I did not need them, that there was nothing in them I didn't already know about myself or life. For I knew it all. It was she who was blind and naïve. She could not possibly know what it was like to be in my place, to walk in my shoes. There is truth to that. She could not know what my burdens were like, but she did know the way out. She was refusing to give up on me. She was trying to give me the joy and gratitude that were in her heart. She held the answers, but I refused to listen.

I had nothing left to give. For me this was the focal point of my life. There was nothing left to give! I was feeling so beaten and bruised – broke, overwhelmed and lost. So much of my life centred on what I could provide, what I had to give. In my youth it was my strength, my carefree attitude. I never thought twice about pushing cars stuck in the snow, giving strangers lifts, stopping at accidents when help was needed, making people laugh, helping them forget about their worries. These things filled me. They made me feel complete. As I got older and became more financially sound, I was able to do it with money. I was driven by a desire to help and the ability to do so filled my cup. The more I gave the more it overflowed. It was an inherent need, nothing valorous or special. Helping others is how we help ourselves, and I knew from a very young age just how empowering and gratifying it was to make a difference. It had nothing to do with a return. There was never any strings attached, that would have ruined it, tarnished it. No, the secret in giving is in sharing your joy and good fortune. The more of it I shared, it seemed the more I had to share. It just kept coming back to me – until my cup stopped filling, until it was half empty and then just a few drops were left.

There was a reason my cup was always full and there was a reason it became empty. As my burdens piled up, as I watched more and more of what I had built disappear, I started to stress about what I was losing. I stopped believing in me, in others. I focused on the ugliness within and around me. I started to fill that cup with anger and fear. Even if I could have found the desire to share from it; it would have been tainted and acidic. Nothing beautiful could survive in that cup.

Today, in this new state of mind, I am reminded of a conversation I had with my sister. It does not hold all of the answers, but I believe it to be in a large part the source of my peace and happiness in my younger years.

She spoke of creating, building, growing. It is these things, that we all do, that give us purpose. Whether it is growing fields of corn, or building bridges, or creating music, we are all capable and at our best when we are adding to our surroundings. It may be fixing, decorating, watering. Something simple or something extraordinary but nothing makes us better than when we are adding to our landscape and embracing our potential. It is this thought that makes me realize part of my depression came from the fact I was not building. I was tearing down. I was not going forward, but rather treading water and looking back at what was lost.

No inspiration comes from standing still or looking backwards. There is no happiness that comes from cutting and slashing. No joy comes from fighting. Even when battles are won, any victory that involves destruction will often be suffered in silence, rather than held high. The misery will always be exposed by the light of day, hollow and without virtue. There is no satisfaction, no feeling of exultation when you stand as conqueror over devastation.

And that was it. I was not building. I was battling, fighting and looking backwards. I was crying over what had been lost, instead of looking forward at what might still be achieved. What was that saying Julie Andrews had in The Sound of Music? "When the Lord closes a door, somewhere He opens a window."

Cherin and I can discuss life on the deepest of levels. We are sisters and our bond is strong. However it is interesting that her spirituality is more new age (Yoga and Meditation). Where mine is more of an attachment to a higher power. We both have our crutch or our inspiration, it depends on how you want to view it. I think in all of us there is a need to have faith in something. It is just a matter of what we can resolve within our hearts to be our truth. Regardless, the end game for both of us is the same – to live a good life without hurting others, by giving, sharing, loving, building, accepting, learning and laughing. Lots and lots of laughing. After all what is more healing and inspiring then the freedom that comes with laughter.

My parents were both very good looking. My Dad with his jet black hair and steel blue eyes that really did twinkle and my petite five foot one and 1/2 (we could never forget the 1/2) mother with beautiful brown eyes and brown hair. They met in Seven Islands, a small little town in Northern Quebec, and married at the age of twenty one. My Mom Sandra, was from Truro, Nova Scotia on the east coast. She was one of four children born to Alfred and Maria MacPhee. Her mother Maria, nick named Rye, was born in Newfoundland. To be honest, I am not sure where my grandfather Alf was born. Mom was a very smart woman who loved learning and had dreamed of becoming a nurse. Unfortunately she was hit with tuberculosis around the age of 17 spending almost a year in quarantine in "The San," which changed the direction of her life.

My father Bob quit school in grade 10, and started working in Northern Quebec and Labrador. He was from Sudbury, a small city in Northern Ontario. He was one of four boys born to Jim and Bernice Rae, whose first son Lawson succumbed to pneumonia as a baby, making my Dad the middle child. Jim Rae, my grandfather, was a heavily decorated war veteran. As a field commissioned tank captain, with the Fort Gary Horse in WW2, he was blown out of his tank twice. The first time he was wounded in his leg and the only survivor. The second time he had to get his nose rewired. I understand that anyone who ever met the man will remember his stubborn streak, I guess you need one of those to get back in a tank after being blown out of it twice.

My grandfather was a very proud man, he carried his Viking and pioneer roots as a badge of honour. Everyone knew Jim was a scrapper. He was not a very big man but he had massive hands. Nobody was going to push him around and what he did not argue with his fists he would plead with a very persuasive pen. Jim passed away in 1991. It has only been in the last few years with all of the talk about PTSD (post traumatic stress disorder) that my Dad has been able to understand the ever more violent side of my grandfather.

My Dad's mother was born in Algoma in 1921. Bernice Hare, but everyone called her Bunny, Bunny Hare. I so loved that woman. Her smile and humour were as endearing as her name. Her grandparents, my great-great-grandparents, were early settlers in the north. Somewhere in this long line of pioneers I have been told there is some Native American Indian in me. I decided a long time ago that with both of my parents families long history in Canada, some of my features and the way I suffocate in crowds, there probably is some truth to that.

Bunny and Jim were living in Seven Islands – or Sept Iles as it is now known when my parents met. My Dad was driving oil tankers across the frozen lakes in Wabush Labrador helping to open up the north. It was dangerous work, as he explained to me, he drove a large barrel on a flatbed truck without stabilizers, over logs thrown and frozen across a lake. When it started to thaw on top, you had to inch your way, hold your breath and pray. Incredibly dangerous work for a very young man, but in those days jobs were considered opportunities. Common sense and street smarts kept you alive. It was better to work a dangerous job that paid well, than to stay stuck in poverty. Or is that just stuck? Stuck in nothingness, no dreams, nothing to build upon and lift you up.

My brother Greg was born in Sept Iles in 1961. I was born in 1963 not far away in Port Cartier, a once thriving port town where the ships were lined up to carry iron ore to the steel companies in the US. In 1967 my parents moved to Lasalle, a suburb of Montreal, where my sister Cherin was born. From there we moved to a duplex in Pierrefonds west of Montreal to a predominantly English area.

My first school, Stonecroft, was behind the chain link fence in our back yard. I went there until half way through grade 3. One year we had so much snow my brother and I were able to walk over the top of the fence to get to school – hard to believe but true. I liked school and loved my teachers. I was bright enough, as they moved me up a grade in math. I loved math competitions, and I don't remember ever losing one. I think I was born competitive.

When I was eight we moved to Hudson. There I went to Hudson Heights for the remainder of grade 3. I remember being a little lost as they had learned some things like cursive writing which I had not. The following year I switched schools again. I was going into an experimental French immersion program offered in grade 4. Yes we lived in Quebec, but we were not French, so this program was a great opportunity for me to get a better grasp of the language.

Dorion Gardens was in a different city, and it was a fairly long bus ride. With the exception of Math and English all subjects were to be taken completely in French. Even on the playground we were not allowed to speak English. This did not sit well with me. I don't know why, perhaps I had a learning block. I did not like speaking the language and I especially did not like being told in what tongue I was allowed to speak in my free time. No matter how it was presented to me, regardless of the logic, I was not happy about being told I had to speak French.

I have no idea what my marks were like in grade 4. We never had a chance to discuss whether or not I would be going back into the program, as my mother had a major heart attack that summer. I was 10, she was only 34 or 35, but it was serious enough that they were not sure if she was going to make it. My mother was the last person you would expect to have heart trouble. She was a very fit looking woman who did not smoke, drink much or eat anything to excess. They say it was a combination of stress and the Pill that created a blood clot in her leg. It is believed the aspirin my little sister gave Mom when she was sitting at home in pain may have saved her life. This would have been around 1973/74, medicine, the Pill and what they knew about heart disease, and how they treated it, was all very different back then.

We spent that summer having only Dad to take care of us. Mom was in the hospital for a long time and then went away to Nova Scotia to recover and rest. I will never forget seeing a picture of her while she was away. Her hair seemed almost white and she had aged. She was a very different looking woman.

As for Dad caring for three young kids, well it really was almost funny. We ate a lot of Kraft Dinner and were thankful when he used milk instead of water to mix it. We ate Alphaghetti, and beans and wieners with toast. Cooking had been Mom's domain. Dad worked and took care of the yard and the car. Groceries were done once a week by Mom, on Thursday nights, when she could use the car and bring along all three children.

To help us through that summer, while Mom was in hospital or away, Dad bought us a puppy. She was part German Shepherd and part Collie. She was so adorable and we named her Taffy for her blond and dark colouring. He was right to buy us this dog. She gave us lots of love and something else to focus on.

It must have been hard on our father. We had no family nearby. Dad's brothers, Paul and Jim, both lived out west in Alberta. My Mom's mother Maria had passed away of cancer when I was five. She was only in her 50s and I still remember sitting on Mom's lap when she told me Nana had gone to heaven. Mom's sister Donna, and brothers Doug and Dave, were all up in Northern Quebec or Labrador.

In Hudson, we lived in an old house with an odd layout. The upstairs was one big bedroom that my sister and I shared. The main floor had two bedrooms and the cinder block basement was cold, damp, and musty. To me it was what history smelled like. When I went down into that basement, I felt like I was going back in time. I often thought I would find some hidden treasure in that house.

One night while my Mom was in hospital I was sleeping in my brother's bedroom off the kitchen. Dad had a friend over and they were drinking beer. The Labatt 50 was out and they were getting louder as the night got on. Usually a funny, happy-go-lucky drinker, that night Dad was beating himself up over Mom's heart attack and telling his friend what a terrible person he was. He started talking about a knife, that I assume was in his hand. He was telling his friend he was ready to use the knife on himself, I lay there praying to God that he would not hurt himself. I knew he was in pain. I was terrified he would do it.

God and I were very close. I could tell him all the things that scared me, and I knew he would understand. He was always there holding my hand, helping me through. Even during some of life's most trying painful moments, I was never angry at God, I was just asking him why? Asking him what it was he wanted from me? I asked him, above all else, to take care of the people I loved.

I could not bare it if he took them away from me.

I went back to Dorion Gardens for grade 5. About all I remember is not understanding half of what I was being taught. I have no idea how I passed. I no longer liked being at school.

In grade 6 when I was 11 we moved again, this time to the town of Pincourt. I think it was partially for Mom's health since the house in Hudson was far too damp and musty, and partially because Dad had found a better job. I know I didn't want to move, but it did seem that things were looking up. The new house had three bedrooms and Dad promised to build me my own room in the basement, so I did not have to share with my sister anymore. I stayed at Dorion Gardens as I had two years left in the four year program. I had a good year, as my grade 6 math and English teacher, Jackie H., was one of the coolest and warmest teachers I had ever known.

My brother Greg was my hero when I was young. As much as we fought – I am sure I drove him crazy – we also had an understanding, "Don't tell Mom". We both had to trust that when one of us did something wrong, the other would not be a tattle tale. There was nothing worse then being a tattler. I am sure that was more for my brother's benefit than mine. He was older, a boy, and way more likely to come up with cool things that were bad. I just came up with stupid things that could have bad outcomes.

Greg had to put up with me, his little sister tagging along. I am sure he hated it, but I wanted his approval so badly that I did everything I could to win it. I remember one year he got boxing gloves, and I was the perfect person to practice on. He taught me how to box, or at least what he knew of boxing and then he would invite his friends over to see who was able to take on his little sister, Did I mention I loved winning?

My sister Cherin was very different from me. She was a girly girl, full of energy and full of mischief. In some ways she was a terror, at least a terror to me. She would break my toys, gang up with Greg to pick on me, and she was always loud. Never one afraid to say what she thought about anything, she was a handful for my mother, and being four years younger than me, I had no patience for her. I resented it when I had to take care of her.

If Cherin wasn't taking my stuff, I swear she was spending her time dreaming of ways to annoy me or doing something for attention. I remember one time she was dressing up one of our dogs, Rinty. It wasn't enough to just put clothes on the poor thing, she decided she would put the hair dryer netting over the dogs head and turn it on. The dog bit her ear and she had to get stitches. I was not sure what upset me more; my little sister's injury or that the dog got in trouble.

After school and throughout the summer, while Mom was at work, Greg and I had to take care of Cherin. Maybe she listened to Greg but she never listened to me. She knew how to get in my head, make me scream, and make me cry. There was the time she went off to the woods and did not come home on time. We were desperate trying to find her, the fear that something bad had happened to her. The hours seemed like days. I do not remember if we had called the police, just that when she eventually came home, she was not stressed, not sorry, just matter of fact. She came home when she was ready.

Another time she pulled the big knife out. I was terrified of what she might do, begging her to put it down, put it away; she just flashed it around and tormented me that she was going to use it on herself. I can't quite place at what stage in our life this was, I think she was nine and I was 13, maybe it was a few months after the the night with the police. She was acting out and had complete control over me. I don't think Greg was there at first but he did show up. Greg may have talked some sense into her, who knew with Cherin. When she was ready she eventually put the knife down and we all swore that Mom would never know about what happened that day. I bring this up because I think it was a moment where we realized how much we loved and needed each other. There was real fear. It was not just a game and we grasped that we, above all else, had to be better for our mother.

We had so much more freedom than kids have today. There are a myriad of reasons I suppose. Regardless, I think it is a shame since so many life lessons are learned through having to make decisions, and make choices on your own, without backup. There are things I cannot believe I did. Yet at the same time there are things I would never do that people tried to push on me. My mothers plate was so full she had to trust us. The one thing I never wanted to do was lose my mothers trust. It gave me the strength not to follow the crowd. Yes, there were times when I was lost and seeking approval, but no matter how bad I wanted it, there were lines I would never cross.

In many ways, I had a pretty good childhood. I loved sports, all sports but mostly ringette (a game played on ice with a stick and a large donut shaped ring) and soccer. I loved pushing myself, I wanted to win, I loved winning. In those days it seemed there was an outdoor rink or two built at every school; one was for just skating and the other for hockey or broom ball. There was always a hockey game to join into with the boys. It was a real source of pride that although I was often the only girl, I was not always the last one picked. We did that then, amongst ourselves we picked our teams, someone was first and someone was last. I never wanted to be last, but I understood when I was. We learned that; how to deal with disappointment, how to accept being the weakest, it's what made us want to try harder.

I think winning is misunderstood. There is nothing ugly about winning. Winning is the achievement. The only thing ugly is what you may have done ugly to get there. Winning is not necessarily coming in first, sometimes it is just finishing, sometimes winning is just taking that first step. It is doing what you thought you could not do, it is setting goals and following through. It is in the goal setting and the baby steps that we find our better selves, that we find purpose, that we find the strength we thought we never had.

Chapter 3

Prepare

*If only I knew then, what a small moment
in time those high school years were.*

*To do it over I would have spent more
time discovering me, and less time trying to
figure out what everyone else expected.*

*Truth is, we were all just waiting
for someone to lead the way.*

It is a Saturday morning in December, and I am at the dance studio. I love it here. Many days I don't just drop my daughter Jodie off and leave, I stay. I watch. The air is filled with possibilities, dreams and beauty. This is where life stands still for me; it is the one place where I can truly live in the moment.

Prepare, it is a word they use frequently at the studio, mostly in ballet. It strikes me as a secret message for life: Prepare, get ready, be ready, be prepared.

Jodie is 15 now, I am watching as her dance is being choreographed, one-on-one with the teacher. They are building, creating, telling a story to music. The director shows her a move; Jodie recreates it. They dance together. They are the same but different. Jodie has taken her instruction. No longer is she the child trying to mimic every move. She has added her uniqueness to it as she extends her fingertips. Her mind and body are now acting in unison. They are no longer just copying. They are interpreting, comprehending and projecting. As I watch, in my mind I can feel myself letting go of her hand. I want this. I don't fight it. The adolescent is leaving my side and the young woman is presenting herself. I want to cry. There is something poignant in this moment. Is this an awakening of her or is it me? Did this just come to pass or did I just become aware? I have always loved and embraced the innocence of childhood, but at this moment I finally see the undeniable beauty of womanhood. I am filled with hope, excitement and anticipation. I can see that she is preparing to fly.

Jodie has danced five or six days a week for years now. She began at the age of six and moved to competitive at the age of eight. It was not what I wanted; it is what she chose to do. To me it was so foreign. I knew nothing about the environment. I had danced for one year, at the age of four, taking ballet and tap. "Pink is for little girls" was my recital song. I don't remember the dance, although I do remember wanting blue to be for little girls too. I was a contrarian from birth. So Jodie chooses dance. In the beginning I fought it and hoped it would go away. It was boring to me. It was lame.

My daughter however, found her passion; her passion is dance. I have no choice, but to accept it, to embrace it. Life is funny. So many things I never knew I wanted, or I needed, have been given to me, even when I fought them. Yes I wanted my daughter to have a passion, but I would not have picked this. Yet here I am fully immersed and embracing dance. I am learning from dance, seeing a different side of me, and realizing yet again, that life can bring us joy and happiness where we least expect it.

When she first started competitive dance Jodie had one number, a duet with another novice dancer. The next year she danced with novice girls a year younger than her. I could see as she watched the girls her own age, how badly she wanted to dance with them. As a mother you want to take away the hurt, yet I also knew to not indulge it. The third year she was still not dancing with her peers. Knowing nothing about dance, I had to trust that the teachers knew what they were doing. It was hard, especially when I saw her watching the dances she wanted to be in. I wanted to ask, to know why, but I stayed out of it. I let her go through it. The only discussion we had was that maybe one day she would dance with those girls. I kept it positive. I would not let her go to a negative place. It made her try harder, work harder, want it more. It was a lesson for both of us. She worked her way to where she wanted to be and found the high and the joy in goal setting and achievement. I found the reinforcing lesson, to not interfere, to accept she will have to go through hurt in life. These are baby steps on how to deal with it. Moments helping her to prepare, learning that she will not always get her way, and that there are disappointments.

We talk about embracing and enjoying the success of others. Encouraging them, cheering them on. There is no room for jealousy, no room for feeling sorry for herself. She gets it, she knows it. I think even better than I ever did. Is it intuitive, is it naturally in her? I don't know. Perhaps a combination of nature and nurture. I know out of everything she needs to learn, knowing how she controls her environment, her state of mind, her view of life, I know this will be helpful as she navigates her way, as she starts her own adventures.

My mother stayed home for our early years. She had occasional part time jobs but for the most part she was a stay-at-home mom. The divorce from Dad changed everything for us. In some ways I was happy to no longer listen to them argue, in others I was sad for the way it changed our life. I missed my father.

After Dad left, Mom found a job as a secretary in Pointe Claire, a city about 30 kilometres away. She would catch a bus before we were even awake and not be back home until around 6:00 pm. I can only imagine what life must have been like for her: Having no car, finding work, leaving the house, finding an apartment and raising three children. The fear of doing all this on her own after her night of terror, and this only about three years after her heart attack.

I remember Mom talking about things like not even being able to get a library card without a husband's signature. She did not want to leave us on our own, but she would not go on welfare. Charity was not an option. Mom was a very proud woman. By example she showed us you don't feel sorry for yourself. You get up, do what you need to do and you don't complain. It was the greatest gift she could ever give us.

The summer of 77 was a difficult one for me. I was going to be 14 come September, and my world had changed. Playing marbles, road hockey and football with the boys was no longer happening. It's what I still wanted to do, but the busy street activity so common the year before was no longer there. Everyone was doing something else.

I started smoking. It wasn't to be cool, I was rebelling, angry at the world and out to prove that I was tough enough. I remember riding my bike to the school one night, not my school but the one my sister attended. My brother and his friends often hung out there. I arrived and Greg was sitting on a low hanging roof above one of the doors. A few of the guys were there and I stopped and lit a cigarette. I must have driven my poor brother crazy. His friends were always nice to me and I wanted to hang out with them.

Greg got on his bike and headed to the store for something. Just after he left another group of guys came along. I didn't recognize them. They were French – funny how this world is. I do not remember any black and white issues in Quebec, instead what we had were the French and English. Just like Ireland had Catholics and Protestants. There is something about humanity where we are always in a battle over differences, be it thoughts, looks, language or religion.

I moved just to the edge of the pavement, close enough to see and hear, but far enough that I could ride away without being caught. I was both frightened and curious. There was some talk and then I remember they started beating up on one of Greg's friends. I think his name was David. Did they smash his head against the wall or has my mind made that up? I mostly remember no one defended David. I could not understand. I thought there would be a fight, then it seemed, as quickly as it started, they left. I asked Greg when he returned why his friends didn't fight back? He told me the French gang had knives. Knives. So many people I know recoil at the sight of a gun, not me. For me it is the knife that brings me fear. It is far more violent. The action of using it requires a far more pointed hate and anger.

One of my best friends in those days was Joey. I did have girlfriends but Joey and I loved playing all sports. That was our commonality. We were constantly throwing a ball or riding our bikes. Children all mature at a different pace, and I was in no rush to grow up. I didn't like what I perceived to be the life of being a woman. I will never forget walking behind Joey's house and him stopping and putting his arms around me. He said something about wanting to do that for so long, and I, being so caught off guard reacted in the worst possible way. I may not have said "Oh gross," but it was probably something close to that. I can only imagine how I must have made him feel. I know I spent a long time wanting to take it back, but I was not in the same head space as Joey was at the time.

The incident changed my world. I lost Joey. I lost a friend. I hated growing up, it was ruining everything.

We stayed in Pincourt until the summer of 78, when Mom decided she needed to move closer to work. I was not happy. Being a child I did not appreciate how difficult the commute to work was for Mom. All I knew was that I was going to have to change schools again. I had finally settled in to a school I loved. MacDonald High School was perfect, I had met some friends I really liked, and now for grade 10, we were heading to a completely different city. The apartment was nowhere near as nice as the one we left. They were called the Pardo apartments, and everyone knew it was where the poor people and druggies lived. The only good thing about them was they were across the street from my new high school. I could stay in bed until the last minute. I was always late for school.

My Mom shared a room with my sister, so I could have my own room. She had a way of making the three of us know we were loved equally, and at the same time she was able to understand our unique needs. Having my own room again was her way of trying to make up for asking me to change schools, It was not the change that was hurting me, it was the timing. Grade 10 is a hard time to make new friends.

My Mom's sister and brother-in-law, Donna and Ken, sent Mom an old Volkswagen from their home in Wabush, Labrador/ Newfoundland. For the longest time we kept the Newfoundland plates on it. Mom did not know how to drive stick shift, so for the first few months that car seemed like it was hopping when she drove it. We used to affectionately call it the Newfy joke. I am sure for Mom, no matter how silly she looked, it was heaven to have a car again.

Mom really was a remarkable woman. She could always make a good meal out of an empty fridge. She was meticulous about a clean house, never ever talked bad about our father and always scraped together enough money for us to have some activities. I do remember her laughing and joking. Times were hard and I am sure she was lonely, but she tried to never let on to her children.

I could not have imagined getting through those years without my ringette and soccer. I did not like the new school. I had no close friends and I could not understand a word my math teacher said. My English teacher was okay; she was my first class of the day. She admonished me for being late all the time, until she finally gave up and just reported to everyone in the class that it must be 8:30 because Wendy had shown up.

By this time my Mom had no control over me. She left for work before we got up and with the exception of gym, drama and English I had lost all interest in school. I believe my math mark in grade 10 was 38%. I suppose Mom could have taken my sports away until my school grades improved, but thankfully she did not. I was stubborn and so lost that who knows where I would have turned without them. I believe to this day that had Mom put her foot down, I would have rebelled beyond drinking and smoking. I played, coached and refereed ringette. Sports and especially ringette were my passion. Sports gave me joy and confidence. They filled my cup when all the other parts of my life were bringing me down.

I started drinking in Pincourt when I was 14. By the time I finished grade 9 I had been drunk a few times. When we moved to Pointe Claire I started going to bars with my ringette friends. At 15 I was the youngest on the team, as I often played up with the older girls. In Quebec the legal drinking age was 18. Most of the girls would have been about 17 and I think they forgot how young

I was. Oddly enough, it was the coaches that we went drinking with, unheard of today, but back then it's what we did.

I was a pretty confused teenager: on the one hand I was naïve, sensitive and wanting to please. On the other I was questioning authority and ignoring rules. I could not stand anybody telling me what to do. I would do what I wanted, when I wanted and the way I wanted, which is probably a common theme with many teenagers. I think not wanting to hurt my Mom was all that kept me from coming completely undone.

Towards the end of grade 10 I had discovered a growth on my labia, I was 15, and I was afraid and disgusted and didn't know what to do. At first I thought it was a large pimple and I tried squeezing it off, but that just made it change shape. Then I thought if I ignored it, it would go away. I watched that damn thing grow for over three years. Sometimes it hurt, but I never told a soul. It did not matter that it could be cancer or something serious; I was invincible, I was not worried about dying. What I was worried about was having to show someone my body. It is hard to imagine. My issues with my body were far beyond modesty, so afraid was I of my sexual being that I could never even tell my own mother about it. I felt like a freak, as it grew in size it became harder to push out of my mind, I wore shorts over top of my bathing suit if I wore a bathing suit at all. I suffered: hoping it would go away, trying to pull it off, making it worse, making it larger. It was the size of a large grape when I decided I might take scissors to it, I got as far as holding those scissors and counting to 10. Thankfully I was too much of a chicken to attempt bathroom surgery.

If nothing else, I had the perfect birth control. I was never going to get close enough to anyone for them to know about my additional body part. As it grew my confidence shrank, and I became more self-conscious. There were never enough clothes for me to cover myself up. Body changes and hormones were all happening against my will. I hated growing up.

By grade 11 I started to meet more people at school. It was thanks to my remedial math class, a special two hour class for those of us who could not follow the mainstream program. We had an awesome teacher and my 38% in grade 10, became an 83 in grade 11. My mother never allowed us to use the words dummy or stupid. I never thought I was stupid, I actually thought I was pretty smart in some ways, but being able to grasp math again went a long way towards rebuilding some of my confidence. Of course that was minus the fact I was a freak with an extra body part.

As was my world, when I got back on track with math, I fell off the bus in history. In grade 10 I kind of liked Canadian History and had a good teacher, so I signed up for grade 11 World History. I was so bored or lost that I spent my class time doodling, I have such terrible drawing skills that even stick people are hard for me so what did I choose to draw? Why swastikas of course! I had no idea what they were, but they were in my history book and I loved to draw them, I put them everywhere: on my binders, on my locker. They became my trademark, and I was totally oblivious to their significance. I was just doodling something I could draw. I was done with school, I had blocked everything out. I could no longer learn, no longer hear, I needed to move on.

Later in life when I discovered my thirst for learning – all of the things I never cared about in school – I realized how offensive those swastikas were. I felt terrible. I was mortified as my intentions were never mean. It was a good example of how easily we can be misunderstood. It helped me develop and maintain my belief that we should never jump to the bottom when we are assessing people and situations. I always give people the benefit of the doubt. It has served me well. I would rather give someone the benefit of my goodwill and have it abused, than not give it when it is needed, as most people truly are just misunderstood.

When I was growing up in Quebec you graduated from high school in grade 11 and then went to Cegep for two years. Afterwards you either went to college or university. It was the last few months of grade 11, leading up to the prom, when I was invited to join a group of girls going to someone's house after school. There were four of us. These were the pretty girls and they were inviting me to join them. I remember having such a great time, laughing, and being silly. They thought I was funny and really nice, and they told me I was pretty – something I had never heard before. We talked about what we would wear to the prom, although I had no idea what I would wear and if I would even go, so I just listened and drank it all up. I was so happy to be a part of this group, and for the last few months they invited me to many things.

I lived in overalls, lumber jackets and sweat shirts. My hair was incredibly straight and I just let it hang. I had no idea what to do with it other then have bangs in my eyes so I could hide behind them. Hanging with these girls made me want to change, at least a bit. As my final good bye to high school, I wore a dress for my yearbook picture and stuck a rose in my mouth. It was so unlike me and in my mind the perfect statement. Everything about my life was a contradiction, so might as well leave school with a big one.

It was never that I could not make friends; I always made friends. I could insert myself anywhere because a part of me could relate to anyone. From a very young age I would stand up for others. I could always – actually I could not help but – sympathize with the other side. I was always advocating for those who were not there, never content to let an unkind word sit as the only truth, as if that were all a person was made of. It was me. I was the one they were whispering about, filled with imperfections, not bad intentions just imperfections. It was not that I was more virtuous; it was that I had such a deep understanding of how easily we are misunderstood. I was both too old and too young, never wanting to grow up and yet feeling I had lived a hundred different lives. I was always the youngest in the class, but in many ways I was the oldest. I was just far too analytical. I never met a thought that I couldn't interpret a dozen different ways. Nothing was simple. There was always a greater meaning: a deeper lesson, a bigger truth.

Grade 11 prom came and went, I was 16 and my brothers girlfriend Lynn let me borrow her little brother Mark for the prom, (a bit of an inside joke as he was two years younger than me and my little sister had a huge crush on him). It was our little secret. I wore a long full-length tight-fitting black dress adorned with a few bright flowers and a slit up the right leg. We went to the Kon Tiki my Japanese style dress was actually almost appropriate, although I still felt like a fish out of water. Mark stayed for the dinner part and then left. I know a group of us went to the Old Munich restaurant and then the top of Mount Royal. We stayed out all night lying on the grass until sunrise. Then we drove to Cornwall, Ontario, for breakfast. I couldn't even tell you now who was in the group. I know I had fun, but whatever group of friends I was with, they were moments in time, I had no connections to that school.

The pretty girls all moved on, as they had real school plans, following a path that was going to take them to university and beyond. For me, I had no plans. I was feeling the pressure of knowing I had to decide what I was going to do with my life. The only things I enjoyed were sports, drama and writing. My sports days were coming to an end, for girls there was no professional path, at least not in Ringette and soccer. There were no jobs in drama. I talked about Broadway but I had no idea what that was and although I had a way on stage of making people laugh or cry, my voice was always an issue. It was low and could be called sultry. I guess it would have been more effective if I was tall and sexy. I never talk about it or dwell on it. It just is what it is and so you accept that which you cannot change. Some people liked my voice, but for me I never had to think about it too much as I could never hear it the way others did. I hated that people would sometimes call me sir, and I knew that I could never make prank calls, since everyone always knew it was me.

My mother was very adamant that I grow up learning to support myself. I so clearly remember her words that I not sit back and hope I find some man to take care of me. It was perhaps the most important thing in the world to her that her daughters were self sufficient. Who could blame her? She believed in the fairy tale of getting married and was now trapped being a secretary, raising three children on her own and just scraping by. We were not bad kids. My brother, although incredibly cool, was also very kind. He never tried to control me, but he did look out for all of us, especially his mother. After the Volkswagen was taken off the road, Greg gave Mom his Newport, a big, mean and ugly army green car that we affectionately called the tank. Greg was the type of guy who would never talk of his good deeds, would never swear and never had a bad word to say about anyone. He was, is and always will be a very solid man, true to his code, to his own contract. He lives by the golden rule as well as anyone can, and he also lives life full out. My brother has always known how to have fun and has a mischievous side that can be contagious.

That summer I applied for a government loan to help pay for Cegep. Then I applied for a job at McDonald's. I ended up getting both, so I enrolled in school to take political science (I wanted to save the world) and Shakespearian English because it sounded smart. I also signed up for their woman's hockey team. Nothing excited me more than thinking about playing university hockey.

I started training at McDonald's and was thrilled about a job paying me $3.23 an hour. It was so much better then the $35-$45 a week I earned the previous two summers being a mother's Helper. I loved it; it was nothing like school. Here I learned the harder I worked the more money I made – I liked that. I learned fast. I challenged myself to serve customers quickly, and because I loved seeing people happy, I always tried to make the people waiting in line laugh. I moved up the ladder: crew trainer, crew chief, little raises and bigger responsibilities.

I made lots of new friends working at McDonald's. It was a different part of town and we were a rag tag group of lost teenagers. We had so much fun working together, playing tricks on each other, playing baseball in the summer and broom ball in the winter. We even started going on camping trips together.

School on the other hand was not going so well. Political science was not the great debating class I thought it would be. We had to start with learning about parliament, the BNA act, and all sorts of boring things that did nothing to inspire me. Shakespeare was okay. My elective Tai Chi turned out to be the biggest disappointment of all. I was expecting karate and ended up with some form of yoga class; I was so not into new age anything.

Although I made the women's hockey team, I had trouble with not being as good at it as I had dreamed. In ringette I was always one of the top players, here with girls coming from all over the country and me being the youngest, I had to learn again and accept my place on the roster. It was okay; I liked it. I just didn't like not being as good as I thought I would be. Life was humbling enough, I did not need to be brought down a notch in sports.

When the first semester of school and hockey season ended, I was offered a full time management position at McDonald's. It was as breakfast coordinator, which meant opening the store and very early mornings. I don't think my mother was too keen on it, but I had to follow my heart and I felt happier and more fulfilled earning money, than I did at school. I quit Cegep and started my career.

Not long after taking the position, I moved into an apartment with two of my new friends from McDonald's, Sandra and Terrea. I was only 17. They were both a couple years older, but I was ready. I needed to leave home, not because I did not love my mother, but because I needed to be free. There was something so exciting to me about not having any rules, about being boss of my own destiny.

For a short period, while I was breakfast coordinator, I had to get up at 4:30 am and ride my bike 15 minutes in the dark to open the restaurant. It was a good thing this was in the summer, have no idea what I would have done had it been winter.

Terrea, Sandra and I had a blast our year in that apartment. For me it was like a rehearsal for being a grown up. Terrea had a car and we would go downtown Montreal for dinners or to a great disco by the lake called the Edgewater. The two of them taught me about dressing up, using a blow dryer and applying make up. (Well, I suppose as much as anybody could).

During this period I fell in love for the first time. For the sake of privacy I will call him "Big Kid". He was the most wonderful amazing guy I had ever met. He was so positive and like a little boy thanks to his enthusiasm for life. We did so much together. We both saw life as an adventure and we both had big dreams with no idea what was going to take us there. Only problem was, we were good friends and the feelings of love were one sided, or so I could only assume. I admired him. I looked up to him. I could not get enough of him. He kissed me one night while we were lying on my bed in my room. I had never felt anything like the way he made me feel. However I was an idiot and a freak. He must have sensed it. He stopped and I went along with his choice. What else could I do, but pretend it was a mistake? I would have stopped him anyway. I loved him so much but even if I could have gotten past my chastity demons, I had that growth. It was painful and torture for me, I was desperate to jump out of my own skin and get out of my own way.

The "Big Kid" and I remained friends for a while and then drifted apart. He found a girlfriend and I experienced my first real heart ache. It lasted for a couple of years. I had never known it was possible to love someone that much. At the time I dismissed it as teenage drama, but as I reflect on it today, he really did own my heart.

There were numerous buddies in my life. I related better to guys than to girls, at least as far as interests went. I had no idea how to be more than a buddy. Despite all the things I would not let scare me in life, and how easy it was for me to make friends and talk to people, the one thing I could not do was go out on a limb when it came to my heart. I didn't know how to flirt, and even if I did, I had created my own personal torture chamber where the rational and logical side of me was being held captive by a very confused young woman. The little girl in me that could not resolve the differences between my virtue and my sexual being. Tortured by the ugliness of rape, and never sure which desires and feelings were acceptable in the eyes of God.

God. My religious teachings ended at a young age, moving so often made it difficult to maintain any affiliation with a church. My mother, who at one time taught Sunday school broke from the church over her divorce. Church leaders were incapable of understanding that a mother's first needs are for the safety of her children. All I had were memories of my childhood teachings: the simplicity of God making the little sparrow fly, the all encompassing love and the request to be good. Praying before bed had ended years ago, but the golden rule always reigned supreme in our house. God was always there for me, at least the one I knew as a child. However now at this stage, I could not resolve my conflict as to what God's requirements were in adulthood. The logical Wendy and the spiritual Wendy were at war.

My grown up days in the apartment were short lived. Sandra was dating Mike and together they did one of the most exciting things a young couple could do; they decided they would see if they could start a life together in California. Mike had an opportunity lined up so with that we had to end our days of being crazy housemates. It worked out for them. The last time I heard they had spent years in Los Angeles, until I believe they finally settled in Vancouver.

I moved back home but to a new house. Mom had moved into a nice townhouse with David. My sister Cherin was still at home as she was only 14 or 15, and Greg was living in an apartment with his girlfriend Lynn. Mom and David had met at a health club. After Mom's heart attack she set out to prove the doctors wrong about her remaining years, by eating like a health nut and exercising 3-4 times a week. I must say for us children we had every new health fad and concoction you could possibly think of introduced to us.

David is a wonderful man who treated my mother like a princess. In fact the way he loved her, and took her places, was one of the nicest things to come along in my life in years. My mother deserved to be pampered, to be loved and to live a better life than just getting by. However it was odd for me to move back and have a man around the house. I realized you cannot go back and that this move would be temporary. I was wary that David might take on some father role and try to be the boss of me. Luckily Mom and David had an understanding, he was not to interfere. Being the gem that he is, David never did. Over the years my love and respect for David has grown immensely.

Before moving back home, I was looking at another promotion at McDonald's as second assistant manager. It meant I had to get a car and pass a course. It was funny how seriously I took those studies. Failing was not an option, so learning and passing had a new meaning. I actually cared about my mark, it meant more money and more responsibility.

I bought an orange Maverick with the words Grabber in black across the front, I don't remember what year the car was, 1974 or 75 I think, this would have been in 1982. I remember the car was falling apart. The heater didn't work, so I kept blankets in the back for when I drove employees home after closing the restaurant for the night. Shortly after moving back home, some poor lady hit my car, while it was parked, and had to pay me more money to fix it than what I had originally paid for it. She was so upset. It would have been cheaper to let her buy me a new used vehicle, but my car was cool and it would have been hard to find another orange Maverick.

I finally went to a doctor when I was 18. I could no longer ignore what was controlling me. I knew I could not live the rest of my life like this, but I also could not get past myself. I finally broke down in tears to my brother's girlfriend Lynn. I had been having terrible thoughts and I felt completely helpless. What I portrayed on the outside was so different from my internal turmoil. I was cool, I was funny, but at this moment in life, I was also desperate.

I would like to say letting it out after all those years was a relief, perhaps, but it was horrible talking about it. It was awkward and embarrassing. Even though Lynn's words were kind, she could not comprehend why I would not have done something sooner. I remember feeling like I was going to die from the exposure, but Lynn's call to action gave me hope. She gave me her Doctor's phone number, a female. It was a small something to take comfort in, although it was not going to be easy. She made sure I called her. The relief was coming; I just had to make the appointment.

I met with the doctor and walked away with some antidepressants and an appointment for the growth's removal. I don't recall how long the wait was before the surgery, but I do know I only took the medication for a few days before deciding I never wanted to take that stuff again. I finally told my mother about the growth. I needed someone to drive me home after the procedure. Now that I knew it was not permanent, and that I was not a freak, I was able to find the courage to tell her. I knew how much it was going to hurt her that I did not tell her sooner. I knew how much she would worry and that I could never take it back, but I also finally knew that the only way to go forward was by dealing with issues no matter how uncomfortable or scary. I learned that facing my fear was nowhere near as bad as hiding from it.

Mom was hurt. She didn't understand why I had never told her and she did exactly what I knew she would do, she wanted to see it. I told her no. That was it. That was part of my biggest fear. I knew my Mom would want to see it and I just couldn't show her my body. Somewhere along the line between 13 and womanhood, I had missed a lesson. In my mind there was nothing beautiful about my sexual being, only ugliness and weakness. I could not accept how fragile it made me. It was the one area that I had no control over, knowing that a stranger, without permission could grab hold of this most personal part of me. Darkening my soul, taking something so private, so vulnerable. No one would ever see that deep inside me without my permission.

I was fortunate that it was a benign growth, a cyst. I could never say for sure what type it was because once it was removed from my body, I removed it from my mind. I wish we had Google back then, but we did not, so we live with the choices we make and hopefully, if we are honest, we learn from them. For me, I was no longer a freak, I could focus on growing up, on life and on where it was taking me. My emotional issues were still there but on this visual reminder I had overcome, not the easy way, but in my own way and in my own time.

I have done a good job of burying thoughts of that cyst. Once I established it was not coming back I have rarely thought about it in the last 30 years. It was nothing. It always was nothing, yet I had turned it into my own personal apocalypse. It serves as a good reminder that what we think is insurmountable, may not always be the case, and that we really do have choices. Today I can not imagine why I never told my mother; or at least I cannot completely jump into the mindset of that teenager and truly comprehend the fear that governed the way she was thinking.

As I journey back in time, revisiting my childhood and early adulthood, I realize the one word that best describes who I was, and probably who I am is awkward. In many ways we all are; it is not just me. Those people in the movies, on TV, have a script, the perfect words and the perfect delivery. Everything is laid out for them. But real life has no script. We all have our fears, our moments of doubt, and our own imperfections. In building on what I know, you may think I have more confidence. In some things I am fearless, however like everyone else, there are limbs I am too afraid to climb out on. For some it is public speaking, for others it is to be alone, for me it has been physical relationships. Intimacy was the most frightening word I knew. I would rather have made a fool of myself on a stage in front of hundreds of people before I let my heart be crushed in one quiet intimate moment. The vulnerability of the naked soul, the fragility of the open heart, to me they were much too delicate to be exposed.

We don't always realize the impact we can have on someone's life. Often it is not the big things, but sometimes the simplest of things. Once there was an issue at our McDonald's drive through, I was called up front to help sort it out. I don't recall what happened, but there was a woman in her late 30's early 40's in an expensive sports car at the window. She was not happy about our service. At the end of the ordeal, when it all was said and done, she looked at me and said, "you're going to go somewhere one day".

Those words meant the world to me. By this time I had moved back home and was starting to lose the passion for my job. I could not see myself working at McDonald's forever so I had a discussion with the area supervisor and the head manager. They felt I could advance further, but wanted me to become more assertive, or based on the woman they wanted me to become more like, they wanted me to be a bitch. I couldn't change who I was. I could not see myself being hard on people, being controlling, being disrespectful. I didn't want that. I wanted to advance and be promoted, but I knew in my heart of hearts that I could not be what they wanted me to be.

So that irate customers words came back to me. The fact that a total stranger had told me I would go somewhere one day motivated me to get my life on track. That I still remember it today, 30 plus years later, is a testament to how much of a difference we can make in someone's life with simple words, little acts of kindness, encouragement.

I was back home and re-evaluating my life. I had been transferred to another McDonald's and was acting first assistant manager. I had passed BOC, my McDonald's management course and my next step would have been some higher level training. However it was McDonald's and with my limited French, in Quebec, it would always be McDonald's and there was something depressing to me about that. I knew my Mom was proud of my career. I wasn't standing still, I was going somewhere, but I realized in my heart it was no longer fulfilling me. I needed more, so I up and quit.

I was twenty years old with no idea what I was going to do. I just knew I needed a change. For the next few months I worked waitressing at a little pizzeria, while I tried to decide what my future would be. I was feeling bored and trapped. I needed so much more from life and felt that perhaps somewhere between Missionary and joining the military, I would find my calling. That was the conflict that was me, to serve God or to serve Country. Somewhere I needed to find my purpose. I had no clue what it was, but settling in a house with a white picket fence was nowhere on my radar.

On a couple of occasions, I was told I would make someone a beautiful wife – once by a friend's father and once by a man at the pizzeria. There were many ways to take those words; I chose to be flattered by them. I was confident in my street cred and in my strength, but being a woman filled me with doubt. I was not unhappy being a girl; I fully accepted and embraced my gender. I just wanted to reach higher and raise the bar, I wanted to do things as a woman, not because of, not in spite of. Being a woman was not a curse. I wanted to show that Wendy, the individual who happened to be a woman, could do anything she set out to do, without blaming men or her gender. I just wanted to go out and do it. My womanhood issues were all about: relationships, being true to myself, my understanding of faith and my fear of intimacy.

Towards the end of my days in Quebec I found myself back in Pincourt. It was at a party at Joey's house. I had not seen Joey for over four years. I was excited, wondering would we pick up our friendship again or maybe I would discover he was the one for me all along. The night did not go well, in fact it was terrible and heart breaking. Joey got even with me, and I left knowing I had to make a change. I was ready to hit the ground running. My happiness was not to be found going backwards so I set my sights on a new life.

It is here that my childhood ended and I made the move to Whitby. I left the security of home for the last time and began my adventure. Armed with big dreams: a growing belief in my abilities, the faith that I could overcome almost anything, and the knowledge that I would be okay if I stayed true to me. I was off to find my destiny, I had prepared for it.

Chapter 4

Fly Like An Eagle

Seek Beauty:
It will soften your heart.

This frame of mind, this time of change, this enlightenment – I have been here before. It was during the Whitby years. The incredible feeling that something wonderful is happening, an adventure is taking place. There is no fear for the future, just a desire to keep moving forward, excited to see what happens next.

There is a need to share, such an abundance of spirited emotion fills my soul. The intensity with which I feel everything is magnified these days. Is it because I went so long without joy that I feel it more? Passion has control over me. I cannot, nor do I want to make these feelings go away. They are the reminder that I am alive. There is nothing sweeter than having desires, fulfilled or not. Desire brings me hope. The overwhelming unknown hunger is worth enduring over the emptiness, the nothingness of the recent past.

I remember wondering when I was 44, when was the last time I cried? It was an interesting thought, as I really could not remember crying much in the past decade. The things that were wrong in my life didn't seem so heavy or at least I didn't wear them and feel their weight. I was feeling so happy, so grateful, so fortunate. I felt that maybe crying was something I had outgrown. During my depression however, I found myself crying everyday. I had no control over it. In the beginning I just accepted it as a need to empty the frustration, the sadness, to just get it out. Over time, it became an uncontrollable reflex. I was disgusted by my inability to control my emotions, and I came to despise the woman I had become.

Today I am back to where my tears are rare. When they do come they are usually inspired by beauty, something poignant. This morning I thought, may the next time I cry be in the throes of passion. It was an amazing thought for me. The old Wendy would have found that disturbing.

I think about love and relationships, probably as much today as I did in my youth. My body and face have since been washed with time (gently I hope). The changes are sometimes hard to embrace. However, now I see with a maturity that only time and living could bring me. Experience and knowledge make the need for patience easier to accept. I have no idea what my soul mate will look like. I joke about having just a little side dish, and that right now I am just window shopping. All true as I try to ascertain what I need and want from a relationship. I now know I am not an island, but my need for freedom makes me question my desire for unity with another. I can see it now. It is not that I want someone to lean on, although that might be nice sometimes. I want someone to share inspirations with, to seek beauty with, to build and create with. Not to save me, not for me to save them but together to complete, to fill each other's cup, to become whole and fulfilled.

I am not whole; I know that. I may still be healing or I may be afraid. Maybe it's just too soon. As much as I want to give to and love someone, as much as I am aware that may be my greatest need, I am frightened by the trappings of where I was. Afraid to go back to darkness and hopelessness. I know I will not, I will never allow that to happen to me again, but that knowledge places huge limitations on finding true love. And so I leave it up to faith. Whether I am meant to journey alone or with another I need to learn to live where I am.

The move to Whitby was exhilarating and the beginning of perhaps the most transformative chapter in my life. It was 1984 and I was just shy of my 21st birthday. This was my great adventure, one I was too naïve to be afraid of and where I learned to truly stand on my own.

Whitby is a small town in Ontario, about an hour's drive east of Toronto, and about four and a half hours west of the home I left in Quebec. The population back then was under 50,000, very British and quaint. It was quite different from the suburb of Montreal I had known. Everyone spoke English and the town was noticeably white, not that it mattered or meant anything. It was just an observation I made fairly quickly. There was an ancestral feeling to my new home.

Arrangements had been made to stay with my friend Alicia's older sister, Rowena, until I found a job. I could do some work around her house to earn my keep. I remember it was an older house, maybe a century home, and I was stripping paint and wallpaper from the plaster walls. I actually enjoyed it. Working with my hands has always made me happy. Unfortunately, as with so many people in my past who touched my soul, I lost contact with Rowena and never had a chance to thank her for all she did for me.

I found work fairly quickly, filing and doing relief reception for a company called IHEC (International Home Entertainment Canada) a video company that sold VHS and Beta movies to video stores across the country. Video was so new at the time that when I told my friends back in Pointe Claire what I was doing, some thought it had to do with porn. We jokingly started calling my new life the "Wicked Wendy Whips Whitby "series.

The job was as simplistic as it could get. I stood in a little room and matched picking slips with invoices, then filed them numerically. I will never forget first walking into that tiny filing room and seeing never ending piles of paper. It was overwhelming and looked insurmountable. I ended up loving the challenge of cleaning it up; or maybe it was just that they challenged me to clean it up – then it became a game, a sport, a test to do what looked impossible.

The people at IHEC were friendly and the company appeared to be growing as was the video industry. I was excited about being in such a fun business. Okay, so maybe I was just filing, but I was going to be the best darn filing clerk they ever saw, and like everything I did in life, I tried to make it fun. There was no shame in working and although people would laugh at the level of enthusiasm I brought to the job, and tell me I was crazy and going to be taken advantage of, I ignored their advice. I learned at McDonald's that you get back what you put into things, I had no other option but to build my life from the ground up. I found inspiration dreaming big things while doing simple things. The mindlessness of filing gave me plenty of time to think about how awesome my life was going to be.

My new address was Wendy Rae c/o General Delivery Whitby, Ontario. I could not even afford a post office box. I found an apartment on Main Street, above one of the shops, and I remember standing in that kitchen thinking it was like being Mary Tyler Moore. Well, maybe I didn't have the career or money she did, but I had a heart that was bursting with the pride of knowing I was doing it on my own. The feeling I had standing in that apartment realizing my life was ahead of me and I was free, is a moment I will always cherish. There was no fear, no doubt, just an incredible faith that I was in a good place, the right place.

My rent was $185.00 a month plus utilities. I was being paid $5.25 an hour. Doing the math, my apartment, heat and hydro, car payment, insurance and telephone brought my expenses up to almost $700.00 a month, leaving me just over $100.00 to live on. I was poor, over my head, and incredibly happy and excited to be out on my own.

The apartment had a long narrow entrance, it was like a bowling lane and it housed the only closet. Once inside the next door, there was a living room and bedroom separated by a half wall, a square kitchen and off that a bathroom with an old footed tub and no shower. The ceilings were probably 18 feet high and I loved it! I could breathe in that place, there was no feeling of the inexplicable claustrophobia I tended to suffer. I can feel like a caged animal sometimes, having to remind myself to breathe and stay calm, but not in this place. In this space I was at peace.

I moved in with my only possessions: my stereo and a coffee table my Dad made out of a door. I had a kettle, a little bit of cutlery, and a few dishes. That was it. My new life began as basic as it gets. For the first few weeks I slept in a sleeping bag on the floor, until Rowena gave me a lawn chair. Janet, one of the ladies from work, gave me an old couch and kitchen table that sat two. I remember in the early days my kettle also served as my pot, I would cook noodles, Alphaghetti, soup, and other exquisite meals in it. It was all I needed. I was just finding ways to fill my belly.

Money was incredibly tight and I was not very good at budgeting, I started building up debt on a credit card and maxed it out. I remember times where pay day was two days away and I had no food. Or the worst was when I was going to run out of toilet paper. I would go through the bottom of my purse, all of my pockets and the floor of the car trying to find enough change for a basic necessity. Always though, when my need was greatest, the answer would come. Sometimes a $50 cheque would just show up in the mail from my Mom. How she knew, I will never know. I never told her when I was struggling, but she always had a way of sensing when I needed her.

The day came when my car hit the end of the road. It was a 1977 Thunderbird, a big, sleek beautiful beast. I did not have the money to fix it and it was only a few months away from being paid off, so I sold it to the mechanic for $700 and arranged to get my bike from home. Actually, it was not that car tied to the loan. The loan was for a different car, a 1980 Ford Cougar that I sold to Alicia and Rowena's other sister Jackie, in Montreal.

Jackie had been my grade 6 teacher and was someone I thought the world of. I had been a mothers helper for her for a summer and she was that kind and caring special teacher that leaves an impression on kids. I sold the good car to Jackie, used part of the money to buy an old Thunderbird from my brother, and kept the rest for my move. Jackie had asked me if the car had a lien on it. Since I did not know what that meant, I said no. When I saw her about a year later, she let me know what she thought of my selling her a car with a lien on it. Some lessons hurt more than others. Not realizing what I had done and the difficulties I had caused her weighed heavily on my mind. I never missed a payment on that loan, but also never realized it meant she could never sell the car or truly own the car, until I paid it off. It was a lesson I learned at someone else's expense, and to this day I still beat myself up over it. It is one thing to mess up my own life, but there was no greater shame to me than to hurt another.

After riding my bike to work for less than a week, I left it at the office one night and went out to the pub with co-workers. I got a ride to work the next morning, only to discover that my bike was gone. I was now without transportation and paying for a car I no longer owned. I could have cried, but instead I laughed and moved on. What else could I do? My stupidity in leaving it out and unlocked all night.

Sometimes in life, things happen for a reason. Almost a year later I was really short on cash, more so than usual. I do not remember the circumstances, just the need. I went to the post office that day and there was a letter from someone or some agency I did not know. I opened it and found a cheque for $200. I was being paid restitution for my stolen bike. I never knew it was coming. It was a gift and once again, when my need was greatest, the answer came in the most unexpected of ways. The loss of my bike turned out to be a blessing. It was at these moments, without overanalyzing the way I have tended to later in life, it was these times when I just came to believe that I would always be okay, that I was not truly alone and I was going to be fine.

I do not think I was filing for very long before my first opportunity came along. One of the ladies on the order desk was going on maternity leave, and they needed someone to fill in for her. Her territory was Northern Ontario. They wanted someone bilingual as so many of her customers were French. Coming from Quebec the company assumed my French was strong enough to offer me the chance. Little did they know one of the reasons I had left Quebec was because my French was not good enough. Oh well, it was better than what anyone else had to offer. WooHoo! The job meant more money and a chance to move into the sales office and work with customers. I was both scared and excited. Being the best filing clerk I could be gave me the opportunity. The extra unpaid hours I put in were not the company taking advantage of me, they were me creating an opportunity for myself.

Working on the order desk was awesome, I loved talking to people, and with my Dad living in a small Northern Ontario town I could relate to my base. I did not know much about the movies I was selling, but I knew a great deal about my customers lifestyles. It was not long before they were inviting me to visit their homes and their towns.

His name was Aurèle and he was one of my largest accounts. He owned a video store outside of Sudbury, Ontario, in a little town called Chelmsford. He was a big man in every way and I loved talking with him. Being ten to fifteen years my senior, he became a mentor to me: Sometimes a father figure and sometimes a friend. He was full of thought provoking expressions and we could talk on the phone forever. It felt like this solid confident man, described by a co-worker as a big teddy bear, was looking out for me.

I made arrangements to meet Aurèle on a Saturday for lunch in North Bay, a half way point, meaning a two to three hour drive for each of us. That was a big part of the fun in being on my own. I could do things like just get up, go for lunch and meet a stranger three hours away. I was not in danger, and yes, I was always aware of what I was getting into. I was fearless, cautious, naïve and sometimes stupid, but always wary.

The night before our lunch I stayed up late partying with co-workers. I knew I was going to be hung over and tired for my drive to North Bay. It was innocent, one of the guys from work gave me a little pill he called a bean. He said it was like an extra boost of caffeine and it would keep me alert and awake for the drive. I loved coffee, so an extra caffeine boost seemed simple enough to me.

When I got to North Bay I was a mess. My heart was racing and I was definitely awake. I met Aurèle at the restaurant. It was not a busy place, but even if it had been, I would have recognized him. How many big teddy bears do we come across in our lives? Nothing like a warm and welcoming smile to help alleviate the heart palpitations that were now consuming me. We sat down and I confessed to him immediately that I was out of sorts from some bean I had taken. Aurèle shook his head and knew instantly that it was speed, one of those bad drugs I had heard about in school. I was grief stricken. I did not ever want to introduce any hard drugs into my life. He calmed me down and we settled into a beautiful afternoon of talking about life and dreams.

I had an emotional connection to Aurèle, I admired him and he made me feel good about myself. He was a deep thinker and he was kind. I know he was laughing at me, but never in a mean or condescending way. It was much more lighthearted than that. He had a cute name for me that I cannot remember right now. It may have been "Sunshine." Regardless, Aurèle was a special man and I have always remembered the words he spoke that day, "It's only money and you will make more tomorrow."

How ingenious and simple is that? Simple words to remove all fear when it comes to money. To minimize its significance, to make it powerless over you. Money will bring you instant gratification, and a sense of security, especially later in life. However, as one who has been with and without money, the truth stands in his words. I could lose all joy in my life stressing over the money I have lost, or I can go forward in the knowledge that true peace and happiness come when we spend our time doing, not worrying. I will take it as it comes, earn it as I need it, and do with it as I choose. I have learned the only thing I like about money is the perceived freedom it can bring. Clinging to it and worrying about it has made me a slave to it. So I remind myself today, what Aurèle taught me in my youth, "It is only money and you will make more tomorrow."

Northern Ontario was actually one of the more lucrative sales territories for IHEC. Due to their remoteness, the people fully embraced the video concept quickly and the competition was not spending much time on them. I came up with a plan to book a video premiere at Science North, in Sudbury, a city of about one hundred thousand people. At the same time, I would load a cube van full of movies and drive to North Bay, Sudbury, Timmins and Sault Ste. Marie. I would stop in some of the small towns along the way and bring movies to them, and let them shop from the inventory on my truck.

I was 22 and excited about traversing the north in a giant cube van. Driving some beautiful stretches of highway. The lakes, the rivers and the forests were pristine and beckoning. These were towns we travelled through when I was a young child, on our annual family vacation camping and picnicking en route to Grandma Bunny's. Our 12 to 14 hour drive along the Trans Canada highway would take us from somewhere in Quebec to Iron Bridge, Ontario, population 800.

There were no cell phones back then, and these were certainly not areas where you would want to run out of gas or have a vehicle break down. I never fully grasped the potential danger of my trek until I was fully immersed in it. Driving during the day with the sun shining was heavenly, but at night with no street lights and thick fog or rain, it was a scary drive for a little girl with a heart bigger than her brain.

On a later trip driving in my Firebird, I got caught in a blizzard coming back from a visit with my Dad. The highway was cut through the rocks and I could not see a thing. To stop would have been even more deadly than to keep going. The snow would have buried me and any traffic coming along would never have seen me. I somehow got behind an 18-wheeler. Where he came from I did not know, but I followed his tail lights hoping and praying I would not veer off the road into the rocks. It was the first time I fully comprehended what people meant by a white knuckle drive. It seemed to last forever and I spent the drive crying a little and praying a lot that I would survive. That 18-wheeler was my only hope, my saviour. He was travelling faster than I wanted to go, but I dared not let his lights get out of my sight. When I finally got into a city, I realized the death grip I had on the steering wheel, as well as my foolhardiness. I was literally peeling my fingers off the wheel.

Sometimes you should know when you are getting in over your head, and booking an event at Science North was not something I was equipped to handle. It was very exciting as no one had ever done anything from the video world for the stores up north. At the same time, it was not a huge market, so the 20th Century Fox rep who agreed to supply a new movie for a special screening left the details up to me. I am not sure how the conversation went with Science North, but the long and short was, I had a 35 mm movie and they were an IMAX theatre. It was an important detail

I kind of missed, and it would be like putting a VHS tape in a DVD player. It was not going to work. Kind of like the lien on the car I sold Jackie did not mean a dent. Let us clarify what IMAX means.

The big day came. Customers drove from all over the north to come to our event in Sudbury. Actually, considering how badly it went I had better call it "My" event. I picked up the very elegant and professional Fox rep at her hotel; I was in my giant cube van. We drove to Science North, and upon arriving, I got a little lost and did not pay quite enough attention to my driving. Being so long ago, I don't remember whether I was backing up or turning when I heard that horrible scraping sound. But if you are going to have a bad day, you may as well go all out. Nope, nothing small time for me. That little car I just hit, and put a big gash on the side of, it happened to have Ministry of Transportation written all over it. The Fox Rep (I would rather not use her name) was not amused. I think she was dying inside, after first being picked up in a cube van, and now this.

We found the owner of the car, or at least its driver, and since it was 30 years ago, I think it is safe to say, without anyone getting in trouble that he kindly told me to forget about it. Life can be so good and people so kind!

We entered the venue to see how things were going. Without dragging it out, we had a really good turn out with a little bit of a problem. The rep heard from the manager that they had told me they could not play 35mm, and yet we still shipped them a 35mm movie. Some details are apparently more important than others. What can I say? Somewhere in the conversation – between are you listening and do you hear me? – I had missed an important detail.

Now we had all these people and no special movie screening. One of the local video store owners was kind enough to go back to his store and grab a TV, a VCR and a copy of "Teachers" an older Fox movie. I was so ashamed of my stupidity, I stood up and took full responsibility. I made sure everyone understood it was all my fault. It was hard, but at 22 years of age I took ownership and a big step in my journey to adulthood.

At the end of the day, my trip was a success. Although it took me years to get over my mistake at Science North, inconveniencing all those people and looking like a complete fool, I did manage to sell plenty of movies from my cube van. The clients appreciated the efforts of a young woman bringing the entertainment and the products to them. They accepted a mistake as just that, a mistake. But the intent, the effort and the honest attempt at goodwill went far beyond the movies I sold out of that truck. I built a relationship with my clients, one founded on mutual appreciation and respect.

I made some good friends working at IHEC and established a great mentor in Janet, the sales manager. She took me under her wing and looked out for me, not just at IHEC, but at other jobs throughout my life. She was one of those people you could always count on to have the answers. She was strong willed, not afraid to go to bat for anyone if she believed in them, and she had a motherly kindness that brought so many people to her door.

During my first summer in Whitby, I was out at a bar one night (hey, I was young and that is what we did). I noticed a group of girls in baseball uniforms. They looked to be about my age, so after a little encouragement from my co-workers, I walked up to them and asked if they played ball. Aside from the obvious in their uniforms and after they stopped laughing at my silly question, they told me they played fastball and could use another player. I was in need of a team sport and had played a lot of softball in Montreal. I had to try out for the team and thankfully made it. I now had an outlet, a sport. A place where I felt comfortable; a place where I could let my competitive spirit run free.

Living in Whitby I lost weight and started to find myself. I started jogging and of course playing fastball. The advancements at work helped my confidence, and undoubtedly the independence and freedom of living on my own made me happier. Having so little money also helped. I was limited in what I could afford to eat and vegetables were cheap. I would boil a wide array of them in a large pot, eat this horrible concoction and then drink the water: Warm with dinner and then cold for breakfast. I called it my vitamin juice. Although other people would find it unpalatable, I actually enjoyed it. If nothing else, I was getting more than enough nutrients.

Once my old car loan was paid, I went to the bank to get a loan for a used Firebird I had my heart set on. The bank manager wanted my Mom or Dad to co-sign, even though I had a good record from the last loan. I told her it was not an option. They had no money and were not responsible for me. The manager was not sure what to do, so Janet offered to write a letter of reference for me. I got my loan, in my name with no one else on the hook for it. When there is a will, there is a way. I lived life that way, always trying to find a way, never accepting impossible unless I could see it was impossible. Not because someone told me it was impossible, but because I saw it was. Even at that I would still hold onto ideas and dreams.

Unbeknownst to me, as I was far too young to understand, IHEC was going through some financial or legal issues. To this day I really do not know why the locks were put on the doors. It was incredibly sad as Lee, the owner, had established a wonderful work environment in a really exciting and growing business. It was probably better I did not know or understand, as I would have worried about my customers and probably about me. Instead the older and wiser people in the know had been trying to find us jobs with a Montreal video company that wanted to open a Toronto branch.

So on one day the doors to my beloved IHEC were closed for good, and the next day almost all of us were in a hotel in North York, a 45 minute drive away. There, on telephones, we worked trying to obtain as many customers as possible for this new company willing to employ us.

Over the course of my first five years in Ontario, I worked for seven different video distributors. Each position advancing my career in an industry I loved, until I finally landed a job at Sony. During that time I never quit any of those companies. They either got bought out or went out of business. I don't ever remember being worried or scared about finding work. The economy and the video industry were growing. Not owning very much in the way of possessions also makes life a whole lot easier.

Always analyzing, always aware of my station in life, I remember thinking it is so much easier to live life with very little, than to have much and lose it. I realized I was more sympathetic to the mighty falling, than us little people struggling and trying to get ahead. I hate to think that was some self fulfilling prophecy, it just seems odd how aware I was and how clearly I remember analyzing the thought.

Two of my jobs in those days required working from home trying to build Toronto market share for a couple of Montreal companies. As strong a person as I believed myself to be, living and working alone was a very hard thing to do. With no daily office interaction, it was hard to maintain the balance that comes from communicating with people face-to-face. Thankfully, back then we still conversed by telephone. I could not imagine living alone and working alone with all communication being over the internet.

I remember when I was working from my apartment for Mel Prupas and Associates, I had a meeting in Toronto for which I had promised to bring donuts and coffees. Money was still tight in those days and when I had booked the meeting I had not accounted for my paycheque not arriving by courier on time. It was not the company's fault. It was just circumstance and something I should have tried to anticipate.

On this particular day, I had $10 in my pocket and needed at least $20, as I was also almost out of gas. The thought of showing up empty handed was out of the question. So, I got in my car and headed to Toronto watching my gas gauge and wondering how far I could push it. I finally got to a stage where I knew I had to stop somewhere. I probably needed the whole $10.00 in gas to make sure I made it to the city and back, but the thought of not following through on my promise was not an option to me. So, I walked into the gas station store and bought a scratch and win ticket. I cannot remember if it was $2.00 or $3.00 but it was a foolish thing to do, unless you are crazy enough to live on faith, in which case you believe your needs will be cared for and everything will work out. And so it did. I won $30.00, more than enough for gas, coffee and donuts. Considering I had come to accept I may win at many things except money, I knew there was an outside force looking out for me that day.

And that has been life to me: to try, always try to do right and be honest. To understand that I cannot control everything, and to accept that there will be times when I do screw up and need to believe I will make it through. Things do not always go our way, regardless of what we have done or not done. I had nowhere to turn that day, or no one to turn to. I did however, have faith. It was not a lesson about God supplying donuts, but rather a lesson in faith and believing that things will work out or unfold as they are meant to. Sometimes these little acts are just there as reminders about the importance of having faith. They are little lessons for the bigger days ahead.

Chapter 5

Mr. C

*The search for truth
is the light that
guides me.*

Morals. Ethics. Right and wrong. Where does our belief system come from, if we are no longer guided by religion? Is it government, majority rule, university professors, our parents? What common ground do we have that helps us conduct ourselves? On what do we define truth?

The hubris of each generation is that we think we are smarter and know better than the ones who came before us. We dismiss them at the risk of relinquishing years of wisdom begot through living a life much harsher and more disciplined then we can comprehend. Indeed in some ways we are more evolved, our science is better, our lives are better and our behaviour more civilized. Or are we? Power still corrupts. We still build people into gods and we have in some ways less respect for the rights of others. We have lost touch with what freedom means. We dismiss the voices and thoughts of those with whom we disagree, not only dismiss, but as vehemently as a pack of wolves, we tear into the rights of others who have a different point of view.

I remember wondering as a child how we humans could have at one time burned women at a stake calling them heretics, witches. How could we send young girls away in shame over a pregnancy? We talk and act like we are above those days and yet we do the same thing now. Those who dare question the science of global warming are dismissed as deniers, uninformed, uneducated. Some would like to see them jailed. Yet all they are doing is pointing out another side and asking for debate, asking for their voices to be heard, as they feel just as strongly that there is a truth to their position. Truth, how can we ever find it if we never allow the other side to speak?

We are not debating the issues. We are shouting down and shutting down debate, removing the freedom of speech that millions of people died for us to have. Churches are not removing rights or convicting people. They are just following what they perceive to be the meaning of the bible; however as with all things subject to human interpretation absolute does not exist. But, they try and they have a right to their views, their journey, and their attempt to fulfill their contract as they understand it to be.

We dismiss an entire congregation over the behaviour of a few worshippers, and all of Catholicism over the terrible acts of a few priests. Have we not learned anything? Who are the haters? It's a term thrown around so carelessly today, it's used to condemn anyone who has a different point of view. Those haters are the people that practiced "Live and Let Live," they are your grandparents and great grandparents who allowed today's generation to live their lives under their own free will. They allowed progress. They allowed people to fulfill their dreams, to love who they wanted and to worship as they chose. What did we do with these sacred gifts and opportunities they gave us, this freedom and free speech? How do we return the favour and honour those who gave us this? We call them haters, we don't allow them the same respect and freedom they bestowed upon us, the freedom they fought and died for. We deny them their free will.

I have not been a member of a church, but I strongly believe in their right to explore, to interpret, to discuss whatever they consider the word of God to be. If it brings someone peace, if it makes them whole, if it gives them strength, brings them love and offers salvation. Whatever needs they derive from it, then that is their contract to negotiate. "Live and Let Live," four simple words my mother shared from her learned wisdom, passed on from generation to generation. If only we would respect the wisdom of those who came before us, or at least try and see it.

We dismiss and abuse our freedom because we have always known it and cannot see how we are losing it. We are still marking people with an "A," or perhaps a different letter, but it is still there. The emperor has no clothes, yet we will not believe it because we do not want to see it. If our minds and hearts and eyes will only see what we want to see, then we shall indeed be led by false prophets.

This is the world we live in today. We put more effort into learning about movie stars than we do about those who control our destinies, and that of our children. I am sure it has always been so to an extent, but our bellies are fuller now, and we can not see how our complacency may end up in our losing the greatest civilization known to humanity.

I am spiritual, always have been. It keeps me grounded, gives me hope, gives me courage and gives me strength. Utopia is a place we search for on an individual level. Happiness can only be felt and comprehended internally, and so it is with peace. When we are all free and understand this most basic of human needs, not to control the lives of others, but to journey with them, to connect, to share, and to fill each other's cups that we may all drink from the beauty that is life on earth.

My guiding light is the search for truth. With every major decision there is a process, The facts must be gathered and from there the issues analyzed. What happens if I proceed this way? What is the worst result? What is the best result? These are the known factors. This is where critical thought is applied to come up with, hopefully, the best choice. Some decisions however, have unknowns. How will others be impacted, how will I be impacted and can I live with the worst case scenario? These are the choices we must make based on our internal understanding of the world around us. Our belief system of what is right and what is wrong. A belief system completely derived by our own journey. At the end of the day, after all of the analyses, if the worst case scenario presents itself, can I live with my decision, and will I stand by and take full responsibility for the consequences? Will I own that? Will I move forward without guilt?

Life is filled with unknowns. We don't know what tomorrow will look like. We have an idea based on the events of today and where we stand, but no one knows for sure what tomorrow will look like. Well, no one knows for sure, if there is or is not a God. You can say you do not believe there to be, or that you totally believe there to be a God. You can no more prove to me that there is not one than I can prove to you that there is. Faith is my crutch. I know that many atheists will call it that. I take no issue with their assessment. There have been many times in my life that blind faith is all I had to go on, so it was the crutch that kept me standing. Some decisions were too big and too important for me to make completely on my own, so faith became the final piece to the puzzle. Is this what God would want me to do? At the end of the day, did I make the choice that reflects my highest self, did I do it for the right reasons, did I put myself in the right order of priority, did I look out for the well being of my fellow man, and did I not trample on the rights and freedoms of others?

I will call him Mr. C because his name is irrelevant. It was long ago, 26+ years. I was still living in Whitby, and Mr. C and I worked together. A very handsome young black man, he was sweet and chatted with me often. We did not have much in common, and I often thought he was making things up just to impress me.

I like to think of myself back then as strong, independent, very rational, heading in the right direction and doing the right things. Yes, I loved to party. I was young and having fun. I was also in an industry that was all about the party, but this event had nothing to do with friends and parties, it was all about an issue in me that had to be faced.

I was happy – incredibly happy. Everything about my world was in some ways like a fairy tale, at least to me. I was starting to make good money and get out of debt, I had made plenty of friends. I loved my career. My mother, brother and sister were now living within an hour's drive. I had lost weight when I moved away from Montreal and kept it off. I felt better about my physical self than at any other time in my life.

I could get in my car, my blue Firebird, and drive out to the country in minutes to get my dose of open air. Quite often I did just that. I drove north and followed whatever road beckoned me. I was so free, so happy and almost completely at peace.

If I wasn't out with friends, I would keep myself occupied by washing my car or going to a park and soaking up the sun. I didn't have a TV, nor want one, so I would try to teach myself how to play the guitar or I would write. I loved music, that was my passion. I loved, loved, loved music. In those days I wanted to write songs. I also had an electronic chess set and could spend hours playing chess, or if my mind needed a rest, a deck of cards would suffice. It really was rare though that I ever felt bored.

I had such a diverse group of friends that on one day I could be with my baseball friends singing folk songs, and the next night I was out at the bar with the boys screaming along to Lynyrd Skynyrd's "Free Bird." I would play cards with my married friends who were home with young children, or I would go to the local night club "Stairways" with another group of friends, and watch everyone dance. I would dance sometimes, but I always felt awkward. I was too embarrassed by the fact I really did dance to the beat of a different drummer. My heart was screaming to let go, but my mind was saying, "Stay cool, don't make a fool of yourself."

My next door neighbours were artists. He was a sculptor and they had just returned from a few years in Europe. With them I was in the world of the Sex Pistols, punk rock and all sorts of stuff to get high on. I never touched drugs, it was their thing. I didn't really care what they did, as long as they didn't try to mess with me. They were fascinating to me. They truly lived free and without any chains. I loved hearing their stories and I loved how they fearlessly approached life. They did try to mess with me a bit, but they backed off when I asked them to. It was always better to be friends with your neighbours than afraid of them and I am happy for the time I spent getting to know them. It taught me a lot about accepting people the way they are, about not passing judgement.

In some ways I saw the world without ever travelling. I sipped coffee and drank beer with so many different people. If you keep an open mind, there is so much to learn from everyone. There was no stress in my life as I had no commitments. Sure I had a job and bills to pay, but I enjoyed my work and my life and needs were so simple. Family visits, baseball games and then whatever

I wanted to do. I just needed gas and spending money. Food was simply sustenance, not entertainment, and possessions were purely practical, unless it was a car. A couch was to sit on, a bed was to sleep on and a light was for reading. Nothing had to look pretty or match. It just had to function.

Nevertheless, I was alone. No matter how occupied I may have kept myself, no matter how much fun I was having, I was still lonely, not every day, not all the time, but enough that it made me question myself. Why, why at the age of 24 had I not ever had a steady boyfriend. What was my record, two, three dates? What was wrong with me? I had men 10 or 15 years my senior, customers, men I worked for, that I knew were attracted to me. Men who had wanted me to meet their families. They wanted to buy me things and take me places. I know two that would have married me. I liked them, and we had amazing conversations. There were so many good things about them, but I couldn't bring myself to be attracted to them.

And then there were the ones I was attracted to, but I didn't know how to act. I didn't know how to talk. Well I did. I knew how to become friends with them. That was easy and it made everything a lot less scary. I thought if I just became their buddy they would eventually realize I actually cared a little more than I let on. Like a John Hughes film, it would hit them and they would know instantly I was the one for them.

I didn't know how to do small talk, and I didn't know how to flirt. I could never trust my instincts when it came to matters of the heart. I lived on instinct, yet here where it mattered so much to me, I had no instincts. I closed up and could not speak. More importantly, I was terrified, petrified that I would go out on that limb, fall and nothing would save me.

"What is wrong with me?" Played in my mind a lot. Although not afraid to live on my own, not needing someone to care for me, I still wanted to be a "couple" with someone. I still wanted to meet my cowboy, my soul mate, my other half, but it just never happened. I didn't want to think about it too much. Who wants to stand in front of a mirror and dissect themselves. Who wants to put themselves under a magnifying glass and look for every single fault? I was not like that. If it was my looks, my voice, my walk, my interests, the way I dressed, so be it. None of those things were changing. I was who I was and not going to try to pretend to be someone else.

Then there was that question swirling in my head, "Do they think that I am gay?" It upset me, angered me, hurt me. I was different. I was awkward. I was a Tomboy and did not like girly things, but I was not gay. I was not attracted to women, in fact the thought of physical contact with another woman was beyond my comprehension. I could not even stand a woman touching me, those huggy feely people that would enter my space. It was one thing if I knew and trusted them, then it was just uncomfortable. But those strangers, how could they not sense, not understand that they were trespassing?

We are all different and I was bothered by the fact that by living the life of me, I was being judged and placed in a box. I was doing it to myself. I knew that. People will think what they want. The need for them to resolve in their own minds where everyone fits is their prerogative. If I couldn't figure it out, why should I expect that they could? Yet I did. I expected the rest of the world to know exactly where I fit. I was incapable of understanding basic instincts, having spent so many years suppressing what I considered to be a weakness, a frailty. An evolved person has complete control over their physical and emotional needs. I would never allow myself to be vulnerable. I needed to stay true to me, to not worry about the thoughts of others. They had not walked in my shoes so they would never understand anyway.

I had made a pact with myself when I was twenty. I don't know why it was my obsession – well actually of course I know why it was my obsession – I just cannot believe it came to this. I had made a pact that I would not turn 25 and still be a virgin. What had started as my belief in the perfect love, meeting my soulmate, my one and only, slowly turned to my shame. It was enough already. It was time to put away those childish dreams and stupid fears, and move on with life.

So one night when I was 24, soon to be 25, I invited Mr. C home for dinner. How I ever became that person, and followed through on that promise to myself I will never know. It was the most courageously ugly thing I ever did. I didn't love this guy. He was just good looking. It was wrong, everything about what I was doing was wrong, but I had to see it through. I was going to get rid of this fear and this fairy tale just like the cyst that made me feel like a freak. Nothing was going to own me anymore. I don't remember much about the night other than hating every minute and wishing it to end. Well, I kind of remember my stupidity in not thinking my plan through a little more. I now had to see Mr C. at the office everyday.

I obviously had issues, but I was who I was, and in life moving forward isn't always easy. Events shape us, but it is our choices, our own free will that builds us. How we accept, own and learn from those choices, that is what makes us.

Did I feel shame, sorrow, disgust, anything? Oddly enough, if I did it was not for long. I think more than anything else, I buried it. I never gave myself a chance to think about it or to dwell on it. I made the decision. I could not undo it, so why give it another thought. Did I think about Mr. C and how he felt? I don't think I was worried about him, after all it was one story he could tell that I knew was true. It was just something I did so I could move on with my life, so I could grow up and let go of my silly ideals, my childish dreams and my irrational fear of intimacy. Was what I did right? Absolutely not. It was awful, but for me it was what I needed to do. I had to give up on the fairy tale, face my fears and put my destiny in my own hands. Unfortunately, I think that may have been the moment when I let go of my faith, unsure if I could trust and believe in something higher. It was here I rewrote my contract with myself, and gave up on believing in true love. I accepted that Mr. Right would most likely be Mr. Alright, and that soul-mates do not exist.

I do know that in some ways life just kept getting better after that night. I moved to a fabulous job at Sony Music, so Mr. C was no longer in the picture. And just a year later I remember sitting in the cafeteria with my new friends laughing about my adventures in dating two really nice guys at the same time.

Sony Music was a dream come true. It was crazy to believe I had a job there, not because I was not suited for it, but because I had wished it. I think it was only a couple of years after I had moved to Whitby that I happened to drive by the building. It was in a pretty area of Toronto on Leslie Street, next to a high-end hotel The Inn On The Park. What struck me was the sign on the building, CBS

Records. I remember thinking could there be anything better in this world then working for CBS Records? I knew instantly that was where I wanted to work. And then imagine, just a year or two later while working in an upstart video department at Sony Hardware, I was informed they had purchased CBS Records and I was moving to that building. I was moving over to the music industry. I was excited beyond words.

Our video department operated under the CBS name for at least the first year I was there. I got the CBS swag, went to the CBS convention, got free music, access to tickets, access to all sorts of amazing things that any 25 year old girl would consider a dream come true. My job was amazing. I was selling music videos and B movies, flying across Canada meeting distributors and talking about rock stars and movies. I went to New York. I went to the Bahamas, I went to Banff Springs and Vegas. I was being paid to travel. This young kid whose family never had anything close to travel money was seeing the country she loved and other parts of the world while being paid to do it. She was being paid to meet people and connect with them.

I had more money. I bought dresses and shoes. I had an expense account, flew first class, stayed in the finest hotels, and was invited to the coolest parties. I was a grown up now. I met some big name famous people, and was given responsibilities and autonomy. I was drinking it up, living the dream. I had arrived.

I remember one night when me, my big hair and my lilac dress were standing in front of the slot machines in the Bahamas. I was sipping wine. Business associates had just left and I was ready to call it a night when Mr. Wealthy Suit walked past me and stopped. He stared at me, looked me up and down and asked me to come join him at the craps table. He was at least 15 years my senior. You could tell he thought he was something special, and he may have been famous for all I knew. You could certainly smell the money and see the confidence. I shook my head no and thanked him just the same. He smiled and persisted, but I held my stance.

I ordered another wine; the offer had been flattering. I was feeling good about myself. He came back, he was smiling and said he needed me for good luck. This time I almost said yes. The adventurer in me wanted to go party at the craps table with the rich guy, but the other me spoiled the party. I was so torn. I wanted to go and feel special, yet at the same time I could not get my head around playing someone's trophy. I left my wine and the casino. I was upset with myself. There was a chance to fly, to step outside my comfort zone, but I was to afraid to take it. Was it fear, was it street smarts or was it just that I knew I did not know how to play the part? I could not be the good luck giggling woman at the craps table. I wanted to be but I did not know how.

Chapter 6

The Eagle Changes to The Wolf

This daughter of mine.
She must have chosen me
So I could learn how to love.

I have a strong resemblance to my sister, more so now than in our younger years. The features were always there. People always knew we were sisters, but she was the thin pretty one, the girly girl, the one all of the boys went after. I was the one the boys wanted to be friends with and I was fine with that. My brother, voted best looking guy in his high school, and my sister the Farrah Fawcett of her day, were perfect book ends. I was never really bothered by it, how we looked was of less consequence than how our early years bonded us.

I am a hopeless romantic. As a child I played with cowboys and horses, Johnny West and Jane, no Barbie and Ken for me. I read westerns. I loved the strong men with incredible moral fortitude and courage, who stood up for right and wrong and respected nature and the people around them. All the little girl toys and stories had no substance for me. Their lives revolved around how they looked. They appeared weak and wanting, with a poor-me edge to them. I had very few role models. Calamity Jane, Annie Oakley, they were women who were different, but so rare. They still found the right man and love, but they found it while being strong, being themselves. What brought me to this, was it environment or nature? Was it having an older brother and wanting to win his favour by being more like him? Was it my family's stories of being early settlers and all the strife they endured? Was it our known, but never documented native Indian lineage? What made me? What makes any of us who we are?

As I wrestle with the young tom boy who was me, I can see where my environment shaped me. We moved a lot, so I had to be strong on the inside to deal with changing schools and changing friends. There were certainly times when my brother and sister were all I had socially. Even at that, my little sister was four years younger, so it seemed she was just a nuisance. It was in dealing with these changes that I found comfort in my strong western men. They changed towns and rode off into sunsets moving on to more adventures and new friends. They were just stories, but they helped me escape. I could relate to the new sunsets and new friends.

"You are not the boss of me" always has been and always will be my greatest strength and my biggest weakness. It empowers me, it keeps me strong, it keeps me from being ruled and intimidated by anyone. You are not better than me. You may be smarter, stronger, kinder, wiser, but like me, you are also human, thus imperfect. You have no right to rule over me. I can choose to heed or ignore your words. I can choose to love you, embrace you, or dislike you, but in all these things, and in all of life, you are not the boss of me.

Unfortunately, it also keeps me from doing the prudent thing until sometimes it is too late. I should have listened a little more to the accountant, to the lawyer, to my life partner Dan, to my friends, to my sister. They gave me some very sound advice over the years. It would have saved me a lot of money, a lot of pain and perhaps a lot of hurt for those around me. Instead, I had to live it to truly understand it. I had to listen to my heart and do it my own way. I cannot fill myself with regrets. The choices I made were true to me, and somewhere in all of this there is an answer.

Self preservation is not just about physical needs. The body is the vehicle that transports me. It is important that it remain strong and healthy, but when we look deep into our hearts and minds, we cannot escape our real truth: our intentions, our convictions. If we followed our beliefs and the outcome was not good, does that make our heart and soul wrong? My battle still continues between the spiritual and logical. Somewhere I know they must be able to walk hand-in-hand. It is finding the perfect balance. Inner peace will not be permanent until I truly grasp this lesson.

Our parents give us life and guide us from infants to adulthood. They help shape us, impart their wisdom, and give us tools to get through life. Then they must let us fly, let us leave the nest and start our own lives. My mother gave me inner strength, she gave me courage and encouragement. All her life she walked the walk, she was responsible, proper, loving and very, very smart. But was she happy, was she ever at peace?

My father gave me freedom. He was always playing, being silly, wearing his heart on his sleeve and trying to spread joy and happiness everywhere. He also has a temper and a wicked stubbornness. You just don't mess with him and definitely you are not the boss of him.

They both had to endure some incredibly difficult times. It was how they approached the lowest of lows that I found some of life's greatest lessons. I love them both. My mother will always have my greatest respect and hold my strongest love, as she was, above everything else in the truest sense of the word, a Mother. She sacrificed, loved us and set an example of how to live a good life. Her self-discipline and inner strength were formidable. She set a bar so high for herself that I felt I could never live up to it, but she set it for herself and not us. There is so much to be thankful for in that, for she knew instinctively that we needed to live our own lives, not hers.

I am more a reflection of my father than my mother; we live life raw, open and free. It is from him that the wild horse runs inside me. The peacefulness of open spaces and freedom beckons. It is the need to blanket our surroundings in happiness and adventure balanced with just enough servitude in our souls, to keep us from coming undone. Both my parents were big promoters of gratitude. They both had a quiet connection with God. My mother was more city: graceful, classy. My father was country and unrefined.

It was in Northern Ontario at my Dad's family farm, or at my grandparent's camp that I felt the most at peace as a child. Fishing, driving a tractor, holding a BB gun, feeding the chickens and collecting their eggs. My favourite part of the farm was the abandoned gold mine. Although I was not allowed to go inside it, I could spend hours sleuthing around it trying to find gold or that clue that gold was still viable in that mine. I did not want to be in the kitchen with the woman serving the men. I saw these positions as forced servitude. I was too young to realize they were necessary for survival and they made sense. These woman often found a way to bring joy into what they were doing. They could not change many parts of their circumstances, but in that kitchen those lovely ladies were cracking jokes and laughing their aprons off. Grandma Bunny and her sisters may have lived a very hard life, but did they ever know how to tell naughty jokes and laugh all day and night.

If there is one thing my mother insisted on from her children, it was to never feel sorry for ourselves. We were not victims and poor-me was not tolerated. Mom was unyielding in this lesson. As a child I did not always appreciate it. There were times I felt I had every reason in the world to feel sorry for myself. It bothered me that I could not wallow in my self-pity. Thankfully, by the time I had left home the second time, I had grown to understand the brilliance of Mom's perspective. I do believe it was the most important lesson she ever taught me. It gave me an incredibly positive and secure outlook on life, and made me realize just how much control I had over myself and how I felt.

—⟋⟍—

I had met Dan on a couple of occasions when I was 26. He was a friend of my brother's from the squash club. We had made a bet on a hockey game. I lost, which meant I had to take him out for dinner. Dan was quiet, with big brown eyes, black hair, stocky build and huge calf muscles. He was a father figure in some ways, a protector. He was harmless and when he drank he just seemed to smile more.

I remember that first dinner. It was at the Keg and with us being so new to each other, conversation was hard. I am terrible at small talk. I can do it for a few minutes to make someone comfortable, but after that I am lost. Words won't come to me. Dan spoke slowly, thoughtfully and different than anyone I had known before. We could be talking about the same thing and on the same side, yet it was like two different points of view. Our approaches to life were polar opposites.

The attraction was simple: he was not threatening, he was gentle, he was good looking to me. He worked with wood, had a good job, liked sports and seemed to be happy. He was a strong man who knew how to fix things, how to build things. He was the alpha male, the cowboy, and he treated me like I was breakable, with respect but with care.

Life is funny. Around the same time that Dan asked me out, my sister set me up on a date with her husbands best friend, Jim. Dan lived in Burlington about an hour's drive west of Whitby. Jim lived in Brockville, about three hours east. The timing was hilarious to me and having them both a distance away suited me just fine.

Jim was not the cowboy, he was the gentleman. He took me to see *Phantom of the Opera* in Toronto. We had a great time and he was easy to talk to. I remember going to his place in Brockville while I was visiting my sister. We just listened to records, talked about music, and life, and planned a golf game. He was a bit of a romantic.

It was so much fun for a couple of months, but then it got complicated. I knew I could not keep seeing both of them, yet breaking off with one was going to be hard. It was not like I was head-over-heels in love with either of them. To tell the truth, I was still just trying to understand relationships and myself. I liked dating. I liked being a couple. The rest was just a learning curve, I figured I should feel something and that it would just come with time.

That was the problem. I knew I was out of time as it was no longer fair to see both. Dan was getting too close and it was scaring me. He wanted more and I just didn't know what I felt. I broke off with him, I had to. He was moving too fast, buying me gifts, being too serious. I broke his heart. I couldn't stand what I had done. I had never broken up with anyone and I was a mess. I had a business trip booked and was going to be away for a week. I think I broke up with Jim, as well. What had started as fun was now torturing me.

That whole week I was away, I could not get Dan's eyes out of my head. I knew he loved me, maybe I loved him. Maybe I just didn't know what love was. I gave into it. I decided the only thing wrong with Dan and I was me. I decided I was probably being too picky, and that no one could ever live up to whatever it was I thought I needed. Dan loved me and would never hurt me. He was safe, he was caring and he was a modern day cowboy.

We moved in together. I moved to Burlington and we became a couple. It was fun going out for dinners with other couples and having lazy weekends, staying in bed until noon and not feeling guilty, or at least trying not to. We would play squash all afternoon and then party all night. Having two people earning money was an added bonus. I had never been able to afford such extravagance, at least to me that's what it was.

I made many new friends at the squash club, a group of woman around my age', and with my brother being the focal point of our relationship, I had family close by. Life was full with so many new adventures, new people, new activities.

Dan was eight years my senior. Many of his friends were eight to ten years his senior. I was in a new world among these people who were established. They had children who were teenagers, closer to my age than I was to their parents. They had houses and money. It was different. I had walked into a new life and didn't see it. I had no idea how much I was about to change. As I accepted the new world around me, I adapted to a different reality. Life became a big party. I no longer needed to internalize, to question where I was going in life. The future was now! It is not that I had said forever, I was just trying it out, but it was fun and it was refreshing not doing it all alone.

I started a new job in Mississauga. The commute and travel

with Sony were becoming too much for me. I didn't like being on the road so much, away from my new life. Sony had become corporate. There was a new President and the mood amongst the people had changed. Everyone was running scared and the back stabbing had begun. No one would admit to their errors or stand up for their beliefs. It's not that I was perfect, just that I needed a family atmosphere and had no patience for the type of games people were playing.

I will never forget the conversation I had with the sales VP at Sony Music, one of the few people for whom I had tremendous respect. He looked at me and said, "Wendy, you do not understand. People do not quit Sony Music. They either get fired, retire or die here but they never quit." There are days I wish I had listened to him, but that is only now in hindsight, as I struggle with my financial future. In truth, I gained so much more from life going the route I chose. I sacrificed security for freedom and for me that meant living.

We were at my grandparent's camp in Northern Ontario when Dan had asked me to marry him. His plan had been to put the ring inside a hole on the golf course', so when I went to get my ball out I would find it. My putting was so bad, he never had the chance. Plan B was after dinner at the cottage. I knew he was going to ask me because I could sense it in his behaviour. I was terrified. I wasn't ready to make such a commitment but I didn't know how to say no.

I never did get married. I was engaged for 24 years. I know I have the world's biggest fear of commitment, but that has to be a pretty big clue that things were not quite meant to be, when everything but the wedding is a priority. I remember saying I had not been to church in over a decade. I would not be a hypocrite and have a church wedding. I remember thinking, if I am not doing this under the eyes of God, then why even have a civil service. Common-law is the same as a government piece of paper, it worked for me. It allowed me to accept the ring without committing myself and taking vows. Nobody was being hurt and it bought me some more time to figure this relationship thing out.

I knew, in fact I always knew, that I was not head-over-heels in love with Dan. I loved Dan. I cared about him, but never the way I should have. I put it down to my being incapable of loving someone. I could not stand in a church and say in front of all of my family and friends, "Here is my partner for life, here is my world, here is my greatest love." So I moved forward loving my life, loving my work, loving my friends and loving Dan as I understood it. Loving all the things that being with Dan enabled me to do. I figured this was my life, Dan loved me and I was too selfish to love anyone, my issues were freedom and fear of commitment. I thought if I could get past those two things I would be able to love Dan the way I should.

It was my 35th birthday when I discovered I was pregnant. Dan and I had been living together for about eight years. I do not remember why I was not on the Pill at that time, I do not remember what possible reason I had for thinking I would not get pregnant. So there I was sitting in my office terrified and upset over this pregnancy. My business was growing. I had so much work to do and I was loving every minute of it. Life was a party and I was so content and happy where I was socially. Why this? Why did I let this happen?

May 29th, 1999, was the day Jodie was born. It was 11:30 at night and she was a C-section. Thank God for that! My fear of giving birth was beyond rational. I was awake and drugged. Her birth was the best high of my life. I was amazed seeing our little girl for the first time, she was perfect. I remember holding her and feeling the magic that comes when a new life enters the world. Nothing, I mean nothing could ever compare. There was no greater high and one of my first thoughts was, I cannot believe I was going to deny myself this! I was not going to have children, but she was and is the greatest gift I never knew I wanted. I also became keenly aware of how much I loved my mother. There was an understanding, a knowledge, an awakening that comes from one of life's greatest events, the birth of a child.

Dan chose Jodie's name; I loved it, I did not know any Jodies at the time, so it brought no images to mind of someone else. There was a song Dan pulled it from, "Jodie stands for freedom." What a perfect name for our child. As I listen to the song now, it is crazy how much she fits the description.

Jodie is an amazing combination of the two of us. She has her father's aptitude for learning, for science, for math. She has a very bright mind when it comes to education. She has her mother's independence and must always do things on her own, without interference. Whether it is at dance or at school, she will handle her own issues. It is her way. I love her for this, I love her strength, determination, persistence, and the way she approaches what she wants in life. She does not manipulate, but debates and uses facts and her mind, to present and argue her case.

Her passion is dance. I call her the anti-Wendy. I wanted her to play hockey, or soccer, or ball, or something I understood. She is a girly girl and I love it. I learn from her. I have learned so much about the softer side of life. I no longer regret her choice of dance, I embrace it. The beauty in dance lifts me, the discipline, the respect and the grace. I now love ballet and the work involved to make it look effortless. It is not boring; it is challenging both physically and mentally. I love the friendships, the silliness of young girls, the closeness and the kindness. She teaches me. Having this little girl has allowed me to see what I never had in my youth.

The birth of Jodie solidified it, no matter what thoughts I had about my relationship with Dan, there was no turning back now. We were married in the purest sense possible, by the birth of a child. This was bigger than a church wedding and more bonding than any legal piece of paper. I was now grounded in my duty as teacher and protector.

Chapter 7

The Birth of Wizbot

If all my faith were in man alone:
Then I would fear the gun,
worship the dollar,
and forever live in the bondage
of society's opinion.

If I were to sit down and take inventory of my talents, my knowledge, my abilities, I am almost certain I would come up with a pretty empty hand. Not a dismal failure, but an offering on paper that would not bode well for future employment. I have no formal education, no impressive skills, no awesome talents, and yet I have been successful. I realize there are different measurements or gauges of success. What was a success for me may very well have been a failure for others, but therein lies the secret. I found happiness with my accomplishments, as everything I was doing was chasing rainbows not fortunes.

So I have limited resources, but an oversized feeling of equality. No one was going to limit me through words. I was too stubborn and too much of a dreamer to be held back. I was everyone's equal, no one was the boss of me, at least not the owner of me.

The birth of Wizbot was not a life long dream. In hindsight it was inevitable, but it was not the original plan. I had left the corporate world of Sony Music to work for Jacob, a larger than life, funny and bright man. I thought I was going to be selling advertising for a video trade magazine, instead it was to sell printing. So quickly was I thrown in the fire, I never even had a chance to realize I was doing exactly what I swore I would never do, work in printing. Printing was my Dad's world, a field I discovered as a teenager, I never wanted to be in. Yet here I was selling printing.

At least it was something tangible, something the clients needed and I could provide. That was my issue with selling B grade movies, it was fluff and circuses. It wasn't rational and my heart was no longer into it. I needed logic and truth, so without any planning selling print became my new trade.

It was not long before I realized things would not work out between Jacob and I. To this day I feel bad about that. It was the first time I ever took a job and realized it was probably a mistake. Jacob was great at many things, but managing people was not one of them. I can say that now, as I realize I have made many of the same mistakes. Dan used to say to me, "You are just like Jacob!"

I started Wizbot in August of 1993. I was 29, a few weeks shy of my 30th birthday. My mother had loaned me $3000. I rented a little office in Oakville for $250 a month, got a cell phone, an office phone and had a lawyer do some name searches. It was a mistake that cost me a thousand dollars I could not afford to spend. I do not like boring paper work but for a thousand dollars I am sure I could have suffered through learning how to do name searches. That was the first of many lessons, the beginning of what I called my collection of ownership diplomas. Certificates from the very real and difficult school of hard knocks.

The business was registered as Wizbot Inc. A crazy name with a long story about trying to come up with something the lawyer was not going to tell me was taken and cost me another five hundred dollars. In the beginning I operated as VidPack Services, I was set up as an agent for a packaging company selling video jackets. They had offered me a job, but the commute to their office on the other side of Toronto would have been insane. I came up with the agency idea and they agreed to it. It was an incredible deal for me, a dream come true.

I remember the excitement and I remember the fear. There was no paycheque. I had no money backing me up except the loan, so I was completely on my own to sink or swim. Dan had been laid off and we had just bought our first home, a townhouse. Finding a down payment had been a creative feat in and of itself. The timing was terrible, but it was an opportunity I could not turn down. Had I been a different person, I probably would have taken the stability of the job; however being me, the opportunity to be my own boss was impossible to resist.

The first year was so hard; I made every phone call I could possibly think of. I had a goal of selling one video box order a day. I stayed focused on that, but it was not easy. The money went fast and the sales came slow. The banks would not help me and I would not ask my mother for more. Every day I made call after call and then bought a scratch-and-win ticket. I tried to draw time out waiting hours for people to call me back. I did manage to start building a clientele. It just took more time than my resources could cover.

I remember the first time I got burned. It was a man operating a charity for pediatric AIDS victims called "Aid to AIDS" The thought of children with AIDS was heart breaking. I remember something about the charity never seemed right to me. It was probably a scam from the beginning, but he was referred and I needed business. I ignored my intuition and decided to trust him. He wanted to create the most expensive cards and letterhead. He was demanding and supposedly rich. He had a beautiful condo in Toronto, a nice car and expensive tastes. I should have listened to the little voice in my head. The one that said ask more questions and ask for money up front. I gave up my only vacation for that project, I worked my butt off to meet his requests. In the end he left me $8-10,000 in debt, an amount too big for me to handle, just when my company was finally starting to grow. My instincts warned me right from the beginning that something shady might be going on. I didn't listen to my internal self, instead I followed the money dream.

Chapter 7 – The Birth of Wizbot

It was a lesson that I needed to learn but it cost me two things. First I had to swallow my pride to ask a friend to believe in me and invest. Second, it cost me 30% of my company as that amazing friend did buy in. I did not resent him the 30%. I appreciated his generosity. I know he could have demanded more. It was the fact I had to do it, that I had to give up a part of my baby that drove me crazy.

I got my first big client in year two, a company with the Canadian distribution rights for "Barney the Dinosaur," I could not have dreamed of a better client. I loved the innocence of children, I loved sappy things, and I loved the opportunity to have Barney in my portfolio. That was my turning point and I knew my future had arrived.

Over the first three years, as I was selling video packaging to movie companies, they started asking if I could do other printing for them. That was the plan; that was my hope. My little company grew, as I started selling design, posters, sell sheets and almost anything else that you could put on paper. It was a recession in Ontario, but it was a good time for me. Computer design was fairly new and I was able to offer the latest technology to my clients by brokering it out. My overhead was low and I worked hard at trying to make money and build a profitable company.

By the third year Dan had started working at Wizbot. We were making more money than I ever dreamed and we were able to join a private golf course, our latest passion. It was so insane and hard for me to believe, it was pretty heady stuff. I was working for it, working incredibly hard for it, focusing on quality and service. The orders were getting larger and more frequent.

Our friend Norm Smith was our corporate accountant. He had started asking half way through my third year of business if I would hire his son. It took some time, as I did not need another employee, but I eventually hired his son Sam in September 1997, the beginning of my fourth year. Sam had a print background and understood how to price it. Dan, who was now doing the bookkeeping, was not happy about Sam coming on board. As he liked to remind me, the day Sam started was the last time he worked there, at least in an office capacity. For me, not working with Dan was a good thing. Although Dan was brilliant with numbers he did not have the print background Sam did, and the two of us were often bickering. I needed to focus on the business and not worry about how my life partner felt. I needed to be the owner and not bring personal battles to the table.

Sam was very bright, dedicated and hard working. He had a big heart, but his biggest downfall was his ego. He always needed to prove himself, and it did not always come across well. His demeanour translated into arrogance, but I could see where it was coming from. He was trying to prove his self-worth against his father's image. His Dad Norm could be larger-than-life sometimes. People either loved him or hated him. You always knew when Norm was in the room.

Sam was eight years younger than me, which was better than my first employee, Brian, who was about 15 years my senior. With Sam I could wear the mantle of boss a little easier. Sam was a hungry go-getter, whereas Brian was a laid-back guy. It was always so awkward asking Brian to do something. I was too young to handle managing him.

That is the freedom part of me. I never wanted anyone to control me and in return I have never wanted to control others. It is a respect for everyone's right to self-determination that made it impossible for me to give reviews, job critiques. In 20 plus years I may have flown off the handle once. For every mistake that has happened, every expensive screw up, I asked questions, followed and tracked the process that created the errors, and then addressed it without being angry at the individual. That was the way I wanted to be treated. We don't screw up on purpose; no one intentionally screws up. If they do it too often we have a problem, but for the most part my employees surpassed my expectations.

In the good days business kept coming. Our reputation grew by word of mouth and it seemed like we never lost a proposal. I loved my job then. It was exciting and fun. I remember dancing on the desks when I landed a new account and always joking with everyone. There was a great deal of laughing and it made me happy. Here was a place of business where people had fun. Yes we had a job to do, yes there were some impossible demands, but we always found time to laugh. We were a team. All of the different personalities, when we worked in unison we were tremendously successful.

From my first 250 square foot office, I moved to 1,200, then 3,500, then 6,000, and finally 20,000 square feet. The bulk of our business was from the entertainment industry doing DVD packaging and marketing materials. That was my background, my network.

Towards the end of 1999, I bought out a small printing company. This gave me a little two colour press and some bindery equipment. I then purchased a five hundred thousand dollar brand new 5-colour Heidelberg GTO followed by a Speedmaster in 2005, worth almost a million dollars.

In my best years, I had 19 employees and we were doing over three million in annual sales. I was giving everyone bonuses: $5,000, $20,000, $50,000. I was paying people well, salaries higher than I ever thought I would earn, let alone pay someone else. I could have kept more for me, but I was not driven by money. It was the freedom. It was the ability to make the rules and run things my way. I was not empire building, in fact there were days I wanted it to stop growing. I was happy with the size we were. I just wanted to create a happy workplace environment, and for the first while I did just that.

It was 2008, I was 45 and had now been in business for 15 years. The early days of wondering where the money would come from were far behind. I was comfortable now in my role as president, no longer the awkward young woman wondering if people would take her seriously. Wizbot was legitimate. My employees had real jobs making real money and for the most part, it was a pretty good place to work.

There are those moments, moments few and far between, where you get a glimpse of what being alive truly means. Those times when you know you have reached the top of the mountain, the pinnacle. The effort, the passion, the achievement all come to be, as you stand in silence, alone, with gratitude and humility. This for me was my Heaven on Earth, where so tiny as an ant I stood and realized the power of faith. The end of a journey I was travelling without knowing the destination. I had kept going against all naysayers, against all odds and around all obstacles. Not prompted by logic, no guarantees in hand, just faith that I had the capacity to navigate by listening to my heart.

I stood in the upstairs mezzanine overlooking my Wizbot world. I knew at this moment I was at my destination, not the final one of my life, but for this chapter in my life. I had accomplished more than I had ever imagined and this one moment was for me. In solitude, I smiled with an overwhelming feeling of contentment, at peace and feeling ever so humble. This is not about forgetting those around you, those that were part of the journey, providing such strong hands to lift you. They are on their own journey and have their own mountain top. This is not ego, this is a testament to the incredible possibilities of life. From nothing and nowhere I had built a business; I employed 19 people. Mountain tops are there for everyone. This was my mountain top and I knew it. I don't know why or how but at that moment I stood in awe and appreciation for I knew I had completed the climb.

And it should have ended there. I knew in my heart of hearts that I was done. I knew that the drive and passion were gone. I should have started working on an exit strategy but instead I became complacent. The building and creating were done, I was now just a manager going through the motions, and not a very good one at that. I was bored but blind to the fact that I was no longer growing and living the life of me.

Outside of Wizbot, life was good, no, life was awesome! I was living a "pinch me I am dreaming" existence for I could not believe my good fortune. I was golfing at a private club and surrounded by the best group of friends my BBG, Beverly Bad Girls. It was insane, crazy how much fun we had. Tuesdays were ladies day. I would leave work at noon, for tee off at 1:00, and never get back home until midnight. We golfed, played card games and head games, match play or anything that made it competitive. We had small wagers and bragging rights and we would be relentless in our rubbing it in.

We had drinks after golf and then dinner, eight of us, 12 of us. The numbers changed, but there was always enough to make it a great night. We laughed; we talked about things I never imagined. We were silly, we were serious, but more often than not we were laughing excessively. It was the best of times for in these years, my early 30s to mid 40s, I found something I had never had before, girlfriends. They offered a feeling of permanency, of home.

I have had many friends, but not like this, with such a depth of affection, trust, and openness. My goodness, with these ladies nothing was taboo. It was so refreshing to spend hours with people that did not judge, or at least not turn everything into character assassinations. Okay, so they did have standards. They were the fashion police and we all knew that leaving early could result in being roasted. Yet at the same time, it was somehow always from a position of kindness and certainly not with the intent to be mean.

I understand people. Moving around so much as a child meant having to constantly make new friends and work at figuring out where I fit in. The experience has made me more accommodating. I do not like the term "a good judge of character," since I work so hard at not judging. I know we all say things we regret, and that for the most part our differences make the conversation more entertaining. I can see a meltdown coming, different styles of communication, looking at the same thing from different angles or expecting someone else to behave the way you would even though what is important to you has no relevance to them.

It is not that I have an instant bond or connection to everyone, that would be far from true. There will always be people that I just cannot relate to, and other people that the attraction is instant. To me it is, and always will be, respect. I do not have to like someone, but I will always and forever respect they have their right to live their own life the way they see fit.

As a child I had no control over my environment. When we moved my friendships ended. You learn that you can go to a new place and make new friends. That life goes on and there are wonderful people everywhere. My mother always talked of the importance of not getting stuck in a narrow vision of the world immediately around you. That staying still will limit your outlook. She was not a fan of small town gossip, she wanted us to see the bigger picture. The bigger world that was our playground.

I have commitment issues: I see it now in everything. If you make a promise or commitment then you have to keep it, far better not to make that promise. I only know that today I want to write this book, I do not know that six months from now I will want to, I don't know that next week I will want to, just that right now at this moment I am doing what I want to do.

I did not see it then, but I see it now. There was an amount of letting go I had to do when our daughter Jodie was born and that allowed Sam, Dave, John and Nicki my new art director now sales manager to set up some amazing systems. Some strong protocols that I never would have had the organizational skills to do. They were amazing at what they did, I intentionally hired people I thought knew more than me. But it also changed the atmosphere of the business. The joy and laughter were replaced by infighting and ego, power struggles and arrogance. I think I was needed to balance things, I may not have been as organized or knowledgeable, I may not have been as ambitious, but I was needed to offset the personalities, to ensure there was respect.

If you want to grow up, really grow up fast, then own a business and employ people. Understand what it is like to always make the final decision, at the end of the day to know that only you can determine the final outcome and that whatever direction you go, you own it. You cannot gather all of the facts and go talk to your boss and say here you go, here is all the info and my recommendation. Nope, you have to carry that weight. If money is lost, if there is no money and jobs are lost. If a bad contract is signed, if there has been a major screw up with your biggest account. If the bank calls, if the government audits, if an account goes bankrupt. If you are short staffed, if the landlord changes the rules and your rent skyrockets. If money is tight, if disciplinary action is required, if a layoff has to happen. All these things of which you were not educated in, all these things of which there is no joy in doing, the responsibility, the ownership can be overwhelming. And you cannot just up and quit, you cannot curl up in a ball and cry, you cannot run away from it. It will make you grow up, it will make you understand what it is like to be the adult in the room.

Chapter 8

The Ides of March

I used to worry about tomorrow,
Until I realized how much it was screwing up today.

For those who have much, much is expected. That was my mantra, my dharma, or whatever you want to call my New Year's resolution for 2010. It was not hubris, not arrogance or ego. It was my gratitude that made me think there was something worthwhile in believing it. So fortunate was I, so incredibly blessed, that it seemed right to want to rise to a new challenge. I was asking to find my higher self.

I needed to give more, and I wanted more purpose in life. I wanted to fulfill my obligations to the world that surrounded me, or God should he exist – God should he exist, so cautious not to fully acknowledge that which many call a crutch, a myth reserved for the uneducated or the brainwashed or the far right conservatives. Yet how do I dismiss, how do I not acknowledge the promise of eternal life? The imperfection of man is so perfect to me in our journey for truth. To write off my Christian faith would be like removing my soul, the foundation upon which my life was built. This amazing journey on earth that may or may not end with the final truth unfolding.

Who is my contract with, in all I do, in every major decision, in each step outside of my comfort zone? When I make those decisions where I am trying to do the right thing, the question always is right for who? Is this right for me, where does my right and wrong come from, with whom is this contract with?

How could I know or even come close to envisioning what lay ahead. It was almost like a curse I placed on myself, as the much that was expected of me became more than I could handle. I can see now how defeated I had become, like some stubborn and irrational fighter, on their knees in the ring screaming incomprehensibly "Hit me, hit me again!" No longer in control of my senses, no reason for why I was fighting. I was flailing aimlessly, punching the air and saying, "You will never take me down." Yet down I was, blind, angry and empty.

I guess clinically they might call it depression, the medical term for what I was experiencing. I never thought in those terms and I never believed I could be depressed. Side tracked, bad day/ week/ year, maybe, but there was never a thought that I could be mentally incapacitated by life. I became earth woman. It was not me that had changed, but the world. All of the chickens from our stupid decisions were coming home to roost. The world was now ugly and I would tell anybody who would listen, all of the asinine things we were doing to ruin what had been a magical place.

It was Tuesday February 23, 2010, a date etched in my mind for eternity. Was it the catalyst of my depression or was it the beginning of my awakening? The writing of this part is difficult for me, not because it brings back any painful memories, just that I no longer want to talk about it. It is done. It was lived, relived and analyzed to death in my mind. I am pretty sure beating a dead horse is the appropriate metaphor, although an awkward one to use in the politically correct year of 2014.

Before I begin, it must be known that I am naïve, or was naïve, or have always chosen to be naïve. I liked the world I saw and lived in looking through my rose coloured glasses. It was a pretty awesome place of mostly happy people and infinite possibilities. It is not that I was so naïve that I lived in fairy tale land, but I did not believe in glass ceilings and for the most part it seemed to me that the world and people were inherently good. Evil existed, but it was people doing evil things from mistaken positions, not evil hearts. I still believe the majority of people are inherently good; however I have come to understand that expecting people to act and behave according to your own moral compass will lead to disappointment. Self-determination applies to everyone! Our evolution requires the voices from many different journeys. We must be allowed to think, allowed to express what we are learning, what we are witnessing. We should be governed under basic laws. We need to be free, yet we need to have a common ground. It is finding the correct balance.

It was late in the afternoon on Tuesday and Sam had asked me to come meet him in his office. I closed the door feeling curious as to what my General Manager had to say. He informed me he wanted to buy Wizbot and that he had some backers. He said he wanted to know what I wanted for the business and pointed out that I was not happy. He suggested that this would be good for me. I could stay home and spend more time with Jodie.

He was right. I was unhappy, but not about owning Wizbot. I was unhappy about the business shrinking and the challenges ahead. I did not want to lay people off and make the hard decisions. It wasn't that I wouldn't, just that I did not want to. I know he said other things, something about his father who was my corporate accountant not being involved in any way, but it was his closing line that left me cold. "I don't want to hurt you and Dan, but if you do not sell it to me, I am leaving and taking half of the business!" Was that rehearsed? Was he serious? Does he have any idea what he just said to me? I was stunned, shocked, beside myself. I always knew he would have to have his own thing one day, I was even prepared to help him get it. Whether or not that would be Wizbot was still to be determined. I always made it very clear that I did not want a partner. I also made it clear I was not walking without some money on the table, not that I was looking at selling, just that if he wanted to buy the company he had to pay something up front. My interest had to be protected – but to threaten me, to think he would need to; why? I could not understand why he said that. The conversation ended there, I could not hear or focus on anything else, I simply said, "Well, I see then", and walked out of his office.

A different woman, a different person would have confronted him right there, not me. I don't know how to react, I don't do knee jerk. I need time to think, to comprehend. I despise confrontation. I question what I am hearing because I don't believe it. There is a pain in my stomach, like I have been punched. Why, after all these years? Why the threat? He knows me better than that. He knows I stand on principle. It drives him crazy sometimes, heck it even drives me crazy sometimes! Does he really think I would sell for less if I am running scared? Does he think I am so stupid I don't realize the power he has over me?

Sam left the building shortly after our conversation. I went to my office to try and digest what I had just been told. Nicki was at her desk working. I was aware but not. I was truly lost and stunned. I went out to the pressroom and stared at the presses. Everything was paid for except the big one, only two years left on lease. How far I had come! All this from a little 14 x 20 office that I rented 17 years ago, and a dream of doing my own thing. I touched each of the presses. I walked up the stairs to the mezzanine where I could look out over my little world. I loved the view and the feeling I used to get thinking I can't believe this is how far I have come. I gave credit, I always gave credit, I always called it ours, I always said we. I was so profoundly aware of how much every employee gave to the success of the company, and I cared, I truly cared about each and every one of them. But it was mine and at that moment,

I was feeling sick to my stomach. I walked back down stairs and into the bindery room. There was a chair by the drill press, I left the lights off, sat in the chair with my head over the table, and started to cry. Quiet sobs that became an uncontrollable flood of tears, I was saying goodbye to my Wizbot. It was not the way I thought I would go, but I was smart enough to know it was over.

Nicki called into the bindery room looking for me. She was leaving and did not want to lock up if I was still in the building. I acknowledged her but did not move. I wanted to talk but I bit my tongue and swore myself to silence until I knew more.

That night I told Dan about the conversation with Sam. Dan and Sam's father were good friends. Dan, although only 10 years younger than Norm, felt like an adopted son. While he was angry he was not as surprised as me. I think he expected it. All I could do was walk around the kitchen asking why, why did he threaten me? How ignorant could he be? Has he any clue how wrong that was? Does his Dad know he's done this? I was sure Norm knew about the plans to buy the business, but did he know about the threat? Maybe it was Norm's idea? They could not be that naïve to not know what they were doing, why threaten me, for what purpose? Sam being Sam has always wanted to show the world he is big man on campus, but not to me. He has never had to play that game with me. I thought he probably regrets it now, so with that I made the decision to give him a chance to take it back the next day.

Sam was outside having a smoke, I went out to join him. I remember how nervous I was, trying to find the right words, so there was no mistaking what he meant. I came right out with it. "Yesterday, when you mentioned that if I did not sell you Wizbot you were leaving with half of it, did you mean Elmwood Pictures and Copy House?" He took a drag on his cigarette and then with a confidant look in his eyes stated simply, "Yes". So there I had it. He had said what he meant to say. I gave him a chance to take it back, had hoped he had made a mistake, but this was it: part of his plan and what I had to work with.

I walked back into the office. I saw Nicki at her desk. We were working on a Wizbot marketing sheet that she wanted me to approve. At the bottom it had my email address as the sales contact, I crossed it off, angrily at that, and said something to the effect of "You'll need to change the contact".

I went into my office and closed the door. Okay, I would have to sell. I had removed myself too much from the day-to-day operations. I may have built the business and brought in most of the clients, but Sam and Nicki had been servicing them for the last few years. They had become the face of Wizbot. Sam had plenty of time to make his plan, and I should have seen this coming. The signs were there. Sam was no longer interested in building Wizbot, he was building Sam.

I had been paying him great money, but it was never enough. I knew that about Sam. He was never going to be happy until he had complete power and control. So where do I begin? I obviously cannot call my accountant for an estimate of what the business is worth, since he's Sam's father. I needed someone to help me through this process. I called Jock, my share holder, and faxed over the company financials. I was defeated and detached. It was all matter of fact. Give me some numbers and I will move towards the inevitable. I was facing a hostile takeover of a private company: Wrong, unethical, immoral, but reality none-the-less.

Jock talked me through the numbers, what he thought the value was and why. He encouraged me and told me not to sell it short. I wrote an email to Sam giving him a dollar figure, and then decided to include in my note a reminder of his threat. For some reason I thought it would be good to have that in writing. I also gave him a deadline of Monday to get back to me with his thoughts. There was no way I was going to keep paying him if he was making plans to steal half the business. I sent the email Wednesday afternoon and waited.

Donna was away on holidays. She was my bookkeeper/ office manager / confidante. I had no one to talk to, no one I could absolutely trust except her. That was the problem, something was nagging at me. I wanted to talk to Nicki but my intuition was holding me back, it was warning me to stay silent and watch. There was something going on and I needed to know who was involved and what the plan was.

On Thursday, Sam left the office to see a supplier. I could access his email from my computer. I always had this ability with all the employees but I never used it. It was my upbringing. People need their privacy and to be trusted, it was just wrong to read their mail unless there was a really valid reason. Even though these were work stations, I never wanted to see their personal emails. This day was different. Sam had threatened me. My company and livelihood were on the line. From my office I opened his inbox and there it was, an email from his father, "Forget that avenue." It was a response. Sam had forwarded my email documenting what I wanted for the business and Norm was responding, "Forget that avenue." What did that mean? To go the other route? To leave and take half the business?

I had no idea what to do next. I decided I would wait for Sam's response the following Monday. His father's email was so brief, with no response or discussion of Sam's threat. Yet it was on my original email, the one he forwarded to Norm. He had to have read it. Was Norm involved? Was the threat his idea? I was driving myself crazy trying to get my head around what was happening. I was also an idiot. I chose not to forward or save the email I had just read. It was not just the thought that it was best I kept my knowledge a secret, it was that I felt dirty reading it. Here were two people I had trusted and cared for plotting to take my business, yet I am feeling guilty reading their communication.

That Friday afternoon I had to leave early to take Jodie to dance. This was her big showcase weekend and it was one of my favourite events of the year. Shortly after I left the office my BlackBerry received an email from Sam. His response to my email outlining what I wanted for the business was simply, "I need to know what you are basing those numbers on." No discussion of his threats, no further conversation, just wanting to know what I was basing the numbers on. He wanted the financials, I think it is funny, his Dad has them but he has to pretend he is not involved. Sam knows as well as I do every piece of equipment and what it is worth, he also knows what is on lease and how long. He knows the sales and he knows the margins. I know what he wants, he wants to see the salaries. He wants to know how much I take and he wants to know what Nicki and John make. Obviously he needs to see the complete picture if he is going to buy the business, but how do I give him this? How do I supply him anything when he has destroyed every ounce of trust I had in him and his father.

I reminded myself that I have to remove this from my head. This is my daughter's weekend, I had to focus on her.

Monday morning I sent Sam the information he wanted regarding how I had estimated the worth of Wizbot. By Wednesday he had still not replied. It had been over a week since Sam initiated this process. I was left hanging in the wind. I couldn't look at Sam, The tension in the office was palpable. I knew now that Nicki was involved in some capacity. She had never been afraid to talk to me, yet she was trying to act like nothing was different. I think John knew as well. Was this a mutiny? Do they all think they are entitled to my business? I couldn't continue paying Sam while he plotted against me, I was ill-equipped to deal with the situation, I had no choice but to contact a lawyer. I needed to know what was or was not legal, I needed to know what I could or could not do.

My mind was full of thoughts of conspiracy. I should have been angry and hurt with the other employees, yet I was neither. I just wanted to gather the facts. These same people who once needed me were now sitting on the fence. They knew what was going on, they just wanted to wait and see who they should align themselves with. I didn't know what to feel. Maybe I would do the same in their shoes.

I phoned my lawyers office and was put in touch with Herb Huffman, a partner in the firm and the employment law expert. I needed to do something. I could not stand watching Sam walk around the office with a giant smirk on his face.

I drafted a letter using some of Herb's legal verbiage and added my own twist. I decided that if I did not hear back from Sam with some type of offer or plan by Friday afternoon, I would give him the letter. My plan was not to fire Sam; it was to warn him. My goal was to stop him thinking he could steal the business. If he was signing leases and buying equipment, he needed to know he had a fiduciary duty to Wizbot. Even though he never signed a non-compete, by nature of his position he had obligations. I also wanted his BlackBerry. I knew he had been communicating via texts and BBM. I could not access those two things, nor was I familiar with them.

Donna was back, I filled her in and she couldn't believe it. Well she could, but it was hard to accept it had come to this. I told her I was convinced that Bert, the co-president of Elmwood was in on it. She believed he was above that. I disagreed. There was no way Sam was doing this without knowing he had Bert on his side. There was no way the other employees allowed this to happen unless he had Bert in his back pocket. I was sure the boys from Copy House were also involved. Sam had been tight with them since the day they walked in. It seemed to me Sam's attitude towards me had changed since he became their friend.

For a week, I paced, at work and at home. I walked around the kitchen island constantly, trying to figure it out. What was he up to? What arrangements were being made? Who was involved? I could not keep paying him if he was planning on leaving with half the business. Why had he not gotten back to me? I could not get past the threat. For twelve years I gave him more opportunities and more money than he ever would have made elsewhere. He had never had it so good. I surpassed the written objectives he once gave me. Who got the bonuses I gave him in such a small company? I remember Dan telling me I was an idiot for giving him such a large bonus. I disagreed. I said he worked really hard for it and I wanted him to know it was appreciated, and that we all share in the profits. What I did not see was what Dan was trying to tell me, it would go to Sam's head. He would think he was irreplaceable and think I was paying him to stay. I would argue with Dan and point out that even I was not irreplaceable, but he did help build the company.

Now I realized Dan was right. For the last two years Sam was out the door at five almost every night. I was not complaining. There was nothing wrong with it. But instead of being happy he was not working so late, he seemed resentful. He was making as much money as me. In fact I had cut my salary to give him the raise he so badly wanted. It wasn't to keep him; it was to help him. But that was not what Sam was thinking. He was thinking the company was nothing without him. What more could I do? He needed ownership; his ego would accept nothing less.

Friday came: Sam had not gotten back to me. I called our security company and explained I needed a witness. I could not ask another employee to be present and I was uncertain as to how Sam was going to react. It was around 3:00 in the afternoon. I called Sam into my office. He saw security and his smile disappeared. I started reading my letter to him; I could not finish it. I was a mess and did not belong in this drama. I left him to finish reading his copy. I told him he was not being fired, but on leave until Tuesday morning when I wanted to meet with him. I wanted him to read my letter, get advice and understand he could not take half the business. I asked him to sign the letter and to relinquish his BlackBerry.

Sam asks me for a paperclip. I informed him the BlackBerry was my property, but he insisted on the paperclip. He says he is not giving me his PINs. I don't know what that is, I think he means his bank passwords. His comment makes no sense to me. I give it to him, I remember my lawyers voice telling me I cannot physically take the phone. I give in. Sam is shaking, opens the back of the phone and does something then hands it over to me. I ask him for his keys. He says they are in his office. As he gets up to get them security looks at me. I nod, yes we have to follow. I know this is bad and that the remaining people in the office will see, but I have no choice. I cannot allow him to do something to my computer.

It was every lawyer's dream, I could see it and feel it but only as it was happening. We had to walk in front of Nicki and Dave to his office. I believe they call it parading the poor worker which was never my intent. I had tried so hard to keep it private and in my office. Not that I was worried, I had not done anything wrong. I had not fired him, despite having every right to fire him on the spot for threatening me.

It was only a short walk to his office. When we entered, I could see him look at his computer and hesitate. He wanted to do something and I said "No." He handed me his keys and I repeated he was not being fired. I apologized again and said I would see him Tuesday.

So much was going on in my mind. I had just exerted power over someone. I hated it, I despised it. I knew Sam better than Sam knew Sam. I knew his strengths and I knew his weaknesses. He came across as arrogant, but everything was an act. His soul was so desperately trying to prove its worth, by living up to the images he cherished in his father and grandfather. Sam was so smart and capable, yet with all that brilliance he failed to see that you can't rise to your best by beating others down.

Back in my office, holding Sam's BlackBerry, I began shaking. I didn't know what to do. What had he done with that paper clip. Could I undo whatever he had done. Why was I feeling so nervous? Why am I shaken up? I wasn't guilty of any wrong doing, yet this phone in my hands felt wrong. It felt like it was not mine, I should not have it. I saw a reset button, or at least what could be one. I wondered if I could undo whatever was done by inserting the paperclip. It was a moment of irrational thought, fuelled by wanting so badly to know what was being done to me. All reason and logic left me. I hit the button and in that brief moment of desperation, I managed to do what Sam could not: I deleted all of the pins, all of the private conversations with all of the players. I knew I had seen red type on his phone and now it was gone. At the time I was not sure, but today I think I did. It hurts me to admit that I personally, in one crazy moment, destroyed all of the evidence I needed.

I started going through Sam's emails on his computer. It was going to be hours of work trying to sort through all of the files and correspondences. It was Friday evening and I was out of time. Jodie was dancing in the first competition of the season that weekend, and I was heading to Toronto that night. I did not want to leave, I was prepared to sit in front of that computer all night, but this was my daughter and this was our time. So I locked up Sam's office and headed out for the weekend.

Monday morning started with another disappointment. On arriving I discovered that Nicki had been in Sam's office and had removed a pile of dockets and papers. She explained that she wanted to take care of any work that was on his desk. Maybe. Maybe not. I regretted not asking for her copy of his key. As trusting as I am, I knew this was not a good situation. Now every empty file on his computer and every questionable piece of evidence that went missing would bring her into it. Sam was supposed to be back Tuesday. I told all of the employees that he was not fired and was expected back on Tuesday. I so desperately wished I could trust Nicki, I wish she had never gone into that office.

I did have one bit of luck over the weekend. There was a text to Sam's BlackBerry from Bert wondering if everything was alright, since he had received a call from me. The texts continued over the course of the weekend. "Sam, are you there?" " Sam what's up?" "Sam I am getting nervous." This last one was everything I needed to know. Why would the co-president of Elmwood Pictures be nervous about Sam not getting back to him about me? How does the little printer make the big movie mogul nervous? It was going to be a good question to ask Sam on Tuesday morning.

The meeting was called for 10:00 am Tuesday morning March 9. I had plenty of time to formulate my approach: All cards on the table, all of the players involved, everything open and honest.

I would start with "Sam, you can buy the business, but not with a gun to my head, not by blackmailing me or intimidating me. Here is what I think it is worth, what do you think and why? What money do you have up front and what are your plans to guarantee I get paid? I know all of these people are involved, so come clean with me."

At 9:50 Donna entered my office and delivered some unexpected news: Sam's mother Betty and wife Candice had arrived. They had gone into Sam's office. I walked into his office just as Betty was calling out for a witness.

"Hi Betty, what is going on?" I asked. She told me they are collecting Sam's personal belongings, as was their right. Confused

I said "Is Sam not coming to our meeting?" Throwing her arms in the air she simply replied "I can't say".

The two of them started talking only to each other as they continued looking for things they claimed were personal and special. I helped them pack. Betty glared at me. Was this the same woman I had vacationed with and Dan had considered an adoptive Mom? I watched in disbelief realizing they knew exactly what they were seeking. Yet it never occurred to me to stop them. I even helped them carry things to the car. Nicki followed me to the door and handed me some CDs to give to them. I have no idea why I did it but I passed them along. Again in the parking lot I asked Betty why Sam was not coming. Her only answer was to glare. I looked at her and said very clearly "He put a fucking gun to my head". Betty and Candice simply hugged each other and drove away in separate cars. I stood stunned. Why was I here? Why was I in this nightmare? Nothing was making sense to me; however I did know what was coming next.

It was shortly after they left that the fax came through, I was going to be sued. This was insane. I had no desire to be at this dance and did not want a legal battle. I wrote a response and informed my lawyer. He advises me against responding, that I should now wait to be served.

March 15th the Bailiff arrived. One of my employees at the time, and a good friend of Sam's came to find me. Was it just coincidence? I will never know but I made sure I showed no fear.

"Are you Wendy Rae?" "Yes I am," "You have been served!" " Why thank you," I replied and then whole-heartedly wished him a nice day.

The Ides of March. How fitting was that? The day I was sued was the Ides of March and all I could think was *et tu Brute*, the famous scene where Julius Caesar discovers his friend Brutus has stabbed him in the back.

Half a million dollars, $500,000 wrongful dismissal. And I laughed at the insanity of this world. I was being sued by people I trusted who thought they were entitled to my business, and even attempted to blackmail me. What did they think? He prefaced his threat with the words he did not want to hurt me. Does that make it some sort of good guy blackmail? Am I a monster worthy of being sued for not knowing he did not really mean it in that way? Did he think he was just being kind and forewarning me that he could do those things if I did not do what he wanted? What type of world do we live in where a lawyer would actually take such a case? More importantly, and I think what was driving me crazy was wondering why his mother or father had not said, "Son, you should not have said that," or "Son, it is not your business to take." Let's face it, even if I was mean, nasty, wicked and evil (which I was not), he still had no entitlement to my business.

So this was the beginning of a very long journey. I had no choice but to defend myself, put together a defence, and go through a legal battle of which I had no want or desire. This was the beginning of my lesson in what it is like to live a life in anger and vengeance. I had finally met my inner demon.

The truth is I could accept almost anything from anyone, being so aware of my own imperfections, my own humanity and my own fears. I could turn the other cheek like no one else, at least I thought I could. I was brought up to never let words hurt me. When someone said something hurtful I was never angry with them. I accepted the lesson and analyzed it. If it was painful I let it go. I could put myself in the other person's shoes and understand why they did something. I have always been able to sense and feel and know. I thought everyone could, but life has taught me that is not the case.

Sam did the one thing I could not turn my cheek to, he bullied me. In doing so I saw what needed to be tamed. My soul could forgive mistakes and I gave him two chances to take it back. Then when he maintained his position to wield power over me, he and his family became my end game. My greatest mission in life became teaching them a lesson.

I documented everything while it was fresh in my mind. I recorded my thoughts, made a list of who was involved and noted my speculations as to how and why it all happened. I knew the other employees were aware, I knew he would have talked to them but I gave them leeway. At first I was angry that no one told me. Time helped me realize they were stuck in the middle. If he had the biggest clients on his side, they had to wait and see which side their bread was buttered on. It did not make it right, but I understood.

I was left fighting a legal battle and trying to run a business where I was constantly watching my back. I did not know with certainty where the allegiances lay. I did have Donna and Jamie who were almost family, so I trusted them. The rest I wanted to trust, but I could not. I was hurting from both the sting of their silence, as well as the change in my heart. I cannot stand mistrusting people.

Donna and I spent the next few months "sleuthing" at night, going through every file on Sam's computer and any evidence the forensic expert managed to retrieve from his hard drive. So many things had been hard deleted. File folders were completely empty leaving me with the nagging feeling that Nicki was involved. We found the email from his father, as well as some excel spreadsheets showing his new company name along with Wizbot's customers. They had been created a year and a half prior. He had been working on this plan a long time. We found many clues that when pieced together told a story, revealing others involved and timelines. I knew this was bigger than what was on the surface. I could see the other players, but I could not deliver the proof. I became certain, in my heart and mind, that there was money being made elsewhere.

Early on, before finding all the evidence, I contacted my lawyer requesting a meeting with the other side. I saw so many people involved and I did not want to see the hurt. As angry as I was, I could see what was coming, and I was still hoping there was an opportunity for Sam to purchase the business. The drama had destroyed my will to remain. Wizbot was now tainted. Sam's dad, the boys at Copy House, Bert from Elmwood Pictures were all going to be dragged into this mess. So many lives would be needlessly harmed if we went any further. We sent a note asking for a meeting "without prejudice." A sit down off the record. What did I get in response to my laurel leaf: A note from his lawyer agreeing to an off the record sit down as long as I brought a big cheque.

The battle began in earnest. I put our golf club membership on hold, and Dan became more active in the business. Between sleuthing and doing more Wizbot work ourselves, we were working crazy hours. The work from Elmwood slowed down. I had conversations with Bert explaining that I was seeking an injunction whereby Sam would not be able to legally do business with him. Bert said he disagreed. On June 30th Bert informed me that Sam had been quoting on his work and Elmwood was moving their business to him. Sam had been quoting on his work. What a joke. Sam knew our pricing and process like the back of his hand. He could easily undercut us as he knew everything we did. We could not afford to lose Elmwood. It was over a million dollars a year and almost half of our business now. I could not believe Sam would do this to the people who used to carry water for him, or at least get him coffee. I realize now, Sam was probably getting direction from the same sources I was. Anger, fear, doubt and ego.

In order to get an injunction to legally stop Sam from going after our business, I had to make a claim against him. So I did something I swore I would never do; I counter sued for two million dollars. It was a beautiful well written claim, outlining the evidence we had gathered. I believed it to be money in the bank one day. I was sure Sam was doing business with Bert and I had convinced myself they were doing business before he left. I also did something crazy; I put the whole legal case in black and white for Bert. I explained that as a fiduciary, Sam was legally obligated not to do business with him. I sent a copy of the letter I had given Sam with a copy of the spreadsheets listing Elmwood Pictures. I informed him that although I did not want to involve Elmwood in any legal action, if they did in fact do business with Sam I would have no other recourse. I blind copied his co-president just in case she was not aware of what was happening. I wanted to make her aware in case there was something unethical happening behind her back. Also because she happened to be a lawyer I felt she might understand my legal position.

A reply came back the next day but not from Bert or his Co-

President Lisa. It came from their head of legal affairs: Elmwood would not be doing business with either Wizbot or Sam.

Well I suppose you could say I burned the bridge, but as far as I was concerned that bridge was already blown up. This was strictly a matter of principle. I don't like bullies and even more I don't like caving to bullies. I just said goodbye to over a million dollars in business.

My summer was spent cutting costs and selling equipment. Some employees left of their own free will. At this stage I had not let anyone go. I found someone to sublet some of our space and I started thinking about selling my big press. Print was in a downturn and I could not digest what I was being told my press was worth. I had figured at least half a million, yet I was being told three hundred and fifty thousand. I was losing – no, I was hemorrhaging over forty to fifty thousand dollars a month. I had been careful through the years to put money away for a rainy day, but this was not a rainy day. This was a hurricane.

I stopped taking a pay cheque and Dan and I started selling RRSPs to live. Life was put on hold while we went through hours of painstaking paperwork preparing for "Discovery" on September 10. It would be the day after my 47th birthday.

In the mean time Dan's routine check up in March had revealed that his PSA level was through the roof, often a sign of prostate cancer. By August it was all but confirmed. He had an appointment with the surgeon September 11. What a special week that was going to be.

I received Sam's affidavit just a couple of weeks before "Discovery."

My lawyer was a genius when he refused to accept the limited information in his first one. The second one was filled with beautiful gifts. Sam's ego got the best of him and in his desire to prove how important he was, his words of self-conceit left no doubt, he was indeed a fiduciary. He also supplied information showing he had been planning his own company on my time, with my clients, and that Bert was aware. I felt there was no way I could lose this.

While discussing my claim against Sam with Herb, the topic of Sam's father came up. Did we feel we might have enough evidence to bring his father into the suit? I considered this carefully. As much as there was definitely some money to be recovered through his father, I could not get past the thought that Norm was only involved because Sam put him in that position. Maybe he went beyond what he should have, but to ruin his practice and his livelihood was not something I was prepared to do. This was Sam's mess, and being a mother I understood how the love and desire to protect our children can cloud our judgment. So I gave his dad some grace.

Chapter 9

Discovery

In a room full of warm bodies
cold calculations were to unfold.
Opening with a harmless pawn
The knight cleverly waiting to pounce.

The end game is always the king,
as the pieces fall in frozen fashion.
Perhaps a single moment of mercy,
A warning to watch the queen.

In a court room setting under oath
The scales of justice tip back and forth,
teeter tottering on each spoken word.
As the masters go about their game,

What piece will they sacrifice next?
What warrior of integrity will fall?
Two souls screaming to tell their story
Two gatekeepers refusing to let it out.

If only I could have seen,
and not been third eye blind.
This was a costly game of chess,
and truth had never been invited.

The cold weather is here. I am afraid of it, worried I may not have the will power to continue walking, knowing my appetite will increase and my energy will subside. It is dark and dreary. I do not want my spring to end; I never want this spring to end.

The need to embrace life becomes almost urgent. How did I go from not caring to almost obsessing about the time I have left? Like a tornado passing through, I was spinning in this funnel cloud of darkness, out of control, watching the damage, feeling the pain and trying to believe it would be alright. And then just like that, the funnel dissipated. It was over. The sun was shining, the air is warm and it was so peaceful. One moment in darkness and the next moment this completely different world. I don't want to ever feel that way again, or is it not feel. I think now it was the absence of feeling rather then the presence of misery. Maybe that is misery: an inability to feel joy?

I can now accomplish more in one day than I remember being able to do in a month just half a year prior. How do I share that? How do I help anyone else find this, or even comprehend why they want to find this? Like the birth of my daughter, the love of dance or love in general, how do you tell someone who has never felt these things, or who cannot feel anything, that it is worth fighting to get there. It is worth the effort and the time spent looking for it; Everything can and will make sense when you arrive. That the answer to your problems does not lie in facing all of those obstacles in front of you. The answer lies in finding you: not the made up you, not the one you project to satisfy everyone else, but the real you, the real you that needs to be satisfied within, accepted and loved by you.

I was not born to live a regimented life fulfilling someone else's idea of who I should be, to behave as others think I should, to act as society says I should. My contract is with me. I have to live with me, be at peace with me, be happy with me. But what defines and teaches me? I have chosen a higher power to be my guide; I believe in God, at least the one I have carried in my heart. I may not know much of what is in the Bible, but I like the wisdom in what I have read. I have not been to a church service in decades, and yet my faith has never been stronger. I was given life. I was given free will. I have been given choices. Why have any of this if there is no object, no lesson, no truth to be discovered?

To live in these times, in this place, in this century is truly a gift, yet it does not come without its own unique set of circumstances. Trying to ascertain what is right and wrong is difficult when the boundaries have changed so drastically in the past few decades. Where religion has become less influential. Our morals and ethics are being written by man, by government, by society. It is not whether or not policy is right, whether or not it can hold up under the light. It is how strong a marketing campaign, it's agenda driven and left vs right. Social or fiscal policy, it does not matter as truth no longer seems to matter. This is what torments me.

How do I satisfy any type of contract with myself and God when I have broken two or three of the Ten Commandments? I was never married. I do not observe the Sabbath and I may have used the Lord's name in vain. I can choose to move forward from this and correct for future, but I do not see myself doing it easily. It is hard to follow these things and therefore I know the lack of religion is not just a scientific argument, but also a lack of will to follow a set of rules we do not like.

So my contract becomes more complicated everyday. I want and need my faith. I need to know that if I spend each day trying to do the right thing, within my boundaries, that everything will work out, that I will be okay. It is setting those boundaries: finding a set of rules/ guidelines that will satisfy my ability to live in today's world, while at the same time appealing to the grace of God. I understand the words gratitude, kindness, love and caring. They are not just platitudes for me. They are the essence of life to me and probably the majority of people I know. I know that killing, stealing and lying are all bad. Everyone I know, knows that. I don't covet. I don't hero worship. I don't feel jealousy. I think this is important. I worry about the influence of Hollywood. I am frightened by the amount of coveting I witness in our day to day lives: by the cries of government, actors and academics to tear down another man's house. How evil is that? Who has the right to indulge the temptation to dictate who has too much and who not enough? I am shaken by the amount of influence we allow these people to hold over our youth. This frightens me; I do not believe it bodes well for the future. I see this as a glimpse of evil that pops up as religion stands down. I do not suffer the judgment of man very well. The old saying "Let he who is without sin cast the first stone," I see an incredible number of stones being thrown and the throwers far from being innocent.

"Render unto Caesar the things that are Caesar's, and unto God the things that are God's". It is a quote that plays frequently in my mind. Since I am not God, then I believe I must be Caesar. Or when do I behave according to Caesar and when is it according to God? I have never been able to fully interpret these words. They always spark a thought process that drives me crazy. The Viking, The Warrior, The Pioneer? Or is it The Child, The Mother, The

Spirit. Who am I ? Do I turn the other cheek or do I stand up for what I deem to be right?

It was September 10th, 2010, I was going to the discovery hearing. Circled on my calendar and forever on my mind the event was an unknown: a place I never imagined I would be. Really, how could I have imagined this. Why would I be in any form of courtroom, in any type of legal drama?

I take responsibility for my actions, I have no desire to gain wealth through questionable or illegal means. I thought I would never sue anyone. I have no evil aspirations, no desire for undeserved riches, no uncontrollable temper. I have an absence of malice. I am simple. I am harmless. The words ran over in my head, "I am harmless, why am I here?"

I was being sued, or at least my company, my Wizbot, and me as the president and founder. I was being sued half a million dollars for a wrongful dismissal. I cannot separate the two, I am Wizbot and Wizbot is me. I did not fire him, and he started it. I was minding my own business, but I had something he wanted, something that was not his to take. Yet I am being sued!

It was a day like no other in my life. I was afraid. Not guilty, but afraid, afraid of the unknown. I was afraid of saying something wrong. I had truth. My guiding light has always been truth, but what if it is not enough? What if I say something wrong. Trickery and traps are always part of TV trials. It's a chess game and I know that. I love chess. My father, now there is a brilliant chess player. My Dad, the little guy from small town Ontario, has played chess masters, and been David against Goliath his whole life. This is my chess game. I am not my father, but I have some of him in me. I know how to anticipate, but a good player needs a strong offence. Here is a place I cannot go on the offence. I am not comfortable here and I do not know the rules.

I am to be questioned first. I am alone even with my lawyer Herb Huffman at my side. I respect him as he is a clever, kind and gentle man. He talks softly and thinks rationally, but I am alone. Only I can answer and only I can bear this consequence. I was not thinking: Mom or Dad or Dan I wish you were here. There is no place to turn, nor am I looking for one. At this moment I accepted the full weight of adulthood. I was alone; this was all on my shoulders.

I was asked if I would mind placing my hand on the Bible? Mind? I was happy to. It gave me hope, strength and something to believe in. Maybe I was not alone. The Bible and the oath took my mind off the ugliness of the event.

His name was Jim Lion. He was a lawyer with the voice of Joe Piscapo and a bit of his stature. We shook hands at the beginning, but after that I was not worthy of acknowledgement. I was a thing, part of a game, and his job was to manipulate me. The irony was beyond belief. The bully had hired a lawyer that was an even bigger bully. It came out over time. It was delicious to watch the bully lawyer bully his bully client: yelling at him, making faces, treating him like a child. As much as I wanted to savour those moments of schadenfreude, I did in fact feel badly for Sam. It upset me that I found myself wanting to defend Sam.

It did not take long, maybe two questions into the examination before I realized I could not stand the man. Perhaps it was the situation, but very few people have ever had that effect on me.

I like people; I will always look for the good. This man filled me with contempt. It was perfect, Sam could not have hired a more perfect lawyer for me. The situation and the examination, this still held me in fear, but the lawyer, he did not. In fact after about an hour, I found myself relishing the moments where I was frustrating him and almost wanted to antagonize him more. He treated me like I was ruthless – like some evil-hearted troll. His vile behaviour gave me strength. I did not have to respect this man. He was admonishing me. I was being painted as the villain and his client as the helpless little lamb. He was trying to beat me through intimidation.

It was Sam's turn to take the stand, I had survived my two plus hours of interrogation. As drained and nervous and confused as I was, I knew it was okay. There were moments when I drove his lawyer crazy, where I thought his head was going to pop. I infuriated him. Those were moments I was able to cherish in the dog days that followed. He gave me a multitude of frivolous undertakings. Each one was requested with a level of self-righteousness, as if to make me sorry for ever hurting his poor victimized client.

I remember thinking to myself: I am only eight years older than Sam. I have less education and fewer resources at my disposal. I don't have the support of professionals like Sam does through his father. I don't come from money like Sam does. Between Sam and all of the people he had involved, there were so many well-connected personalities. Yet, I was being treated like the fire-breathing dragon that must be brought down. It was just so weird to have all of these big influential people wanting to take me down, like they were doing some kind of service to humanity, by putting me in my rightful place.

It was wonderful watching Herb question Sam. Herb is a kind and level-headed man. He put Sam at ease; he was the opposite of Sam's lawyer. Now as an observer of this chess match, it was easy to see who was the master in the room. Herb at one point had Sam come out and admit, "Not Wendy, she doesn't have the heart to fire anyone." I thought that was a pretty good moment in a wrongful dismissal suit.

Jim Lion was not impressed. There were numerous times when he was barking at his own client. It really was not Sam's fault: Herb really was that good and Sam really never had a case. I have always wanted to know if this "Jim Lion" was some ambulance chasing lawyer the 'boys' referred amongst themselves, or if he was Sam's dad's idea. Regardless, I found him quite dishonourable. I am not sure he ever met a rule that he thought applied to him

When it was over, and we were leaving, Sam and I made eye contact. His shoulders were down and he muttered, "Wiz, I am sorry". It was faint and came from a man who had been through hell. It was the first time in my life, I did not accept someone's apology. It was too late for that. Too many lives had been affected by this greed, and these bullies. My heart had been hardened and I could find no forgiveness in my soul.

"Wiz" or "Wizbot". That was my name: my nickname. No one called me Wendy. They called me Wiz, that was how synonymous, how intertwined I was with my company. I am Wizbot; Wizbot is me.

The next day Herb received a message on voice mail from Jim. "So now that you have heard all of the evidence will your client be conceding". You have to be kidding me? Was he at the same event I was? He also boasted about his client doing exceedingly well financially in his new endeavour. Now this lawyer whose client is being sued for a breach of fiduciary duty, is rubbing in my face that Sam's business is doing exceedingly well!

Both those statements threw fuel on the fire. They got me hook, line and sinker. One made me think that Jim Lion was an idiot; the second one made me even more convinced Sam was doing work with Elmwood.

I had my undertakings to put together. Another discovery was scheduled for October in the matter of my claim against Sam. Of course that discovery ended up being postponed until January, that is how the legal system works. It drags on and on and on and on.

Dan and I went to see the urologist the day after the hearing. It was confirmed: He had prostate cancer. The good news was it was caught early and they did not anticipate he would have to go through chemo or radiation. The bad news was it was still prostate cancer. A major life-changing surgery was ahead of him. We did not talk about what that involved. The lawsuit and our financial worries had been controlling our lives over the last few months. Dan and I, well who knows what we were. We just continued as two people struggling, I guess.

That was the hard part for Dan and I. It always was, as we both dealt with adversity in two completely different ways. Dan was hearing the C word and I was hearing an excellent prognosis. He needed more from me. It was hard enough for him already being stuck on the side lines, having to trust I was handling the legal and financial crisis. Now he had to go through this personal crisis living with a person who was in survival mode. I was looking at this as stay strong, keep moving, no time to feel sorry for ourselves.

Dan's surgery was scheduled for November, but October brought more bad news. While being tested for other things, they discovered Dan had aneurysms, not just one, but a few in his abdomen and knees. These were probably a bigger threat to his life than the cancer. So Dan's journey of multiple, major, life-saving surgeries began. A seemingly healthy fifty-five year old man was dealing with multiple silent killers.

I spent the fall putting together my undertakings and preparing my affidavit for January. Business was terrible. I was still trying to deal with an overhead that was way too high for our current sales. We started a government work-share program which helped a bit. I finally came to terms with having to sell the big press, no matter what the price, at $12,000 a month in lease payments and so much work gone, it was killing me. We were now losing about $20,000 a month. It was better than the $50,000 we were losing in the beginning, but I was running out of money.

Demand for print was on a decline. Costs were going up and the shrinking market meant everyone was lowering their prices to survive. The future was not looking bright.

Dan's prostate surgery was successful, at least from the standpoint of completely removing the cancer. Emotionally it was incredibly hard. They had decided to take care of the cancer, before battling the aneurysms. That surgery was scheduled for April and was going to involve an even longer recovery.

January 2011 came along. I was excited that Discovery was coming up. Herb had asked for some undertakings from Sam that

I was looking forward to seeing. But of course, as I was learning, in the legal world the games never end. Jim Lion was a master at playing games. Just a week prior Jim Lion notified us that he had a trip to Dubai, so we would have to postpone. It wasn't right, nor ethical, but Jim Lion did not play by the rules.

Although Work-Share helped, it was not enough. I started thinking about closing down the business, only halfheartedly, as the thought of closing Wizbot was not just the loss of jobs, not just watching my baby disappear, but it would mean that Sam won. The thought of Sam and the boys in a bar laughing about taking me down was more than I could handle. My ego could never accept the boys' club beating me.

In around March, Jim Lion proposed that his client was willing to drop his charges, if we would do the same. I laughed. Of course he is, I knew I was sitting with a full house and he did not even have a pair of twos. It is pretty hard to step away from the table when you think this one hand will solve all of your financial woes. And the financial woes were many.

Jim Lion started telling us Sam had no money. I found that incredibly hard to believe after being told in October he was doing fantastic. By this point, I had convinced myself that something shady was going on with Elmwood Pictures. That was the problem. There had been so many undeniable lies early on in the game from their side, that I could never trust a word they said.

My press was up for sale, but I had waited too long. The bank would not increase my line of credit and I was having trouble meeting my obligations. It was a stupid thing to do, yet I saw no other way out: I took out a line of credit against the house. Considering the only true want I ever had in life was freedom, I hated building debt back against a house that was almost mortgage-free.

Dan was justifiably upset; he was worried we would lose the house. I didn't see that happening and I told him so. I also had no clue what else we could do. We had run out of options. We could close the business, and walk away with nothing, and probably still owe money to the bank. Or we take a chance that things turn around and this step would buy us time.

Dan had his aneurysm surgery in April, in the middle of Jodie's dance competition season. It was a bit much on all of us: Trying to keep life normal for Jodie, dealing with the business and the lawyers, and Dan's recovery. I was not the doting loving wife. I did what was required, but always with a sense of duty. Yes I cared, but I was not worried. I was not nearly as sympathetic as I should have been. I guess the right wording would be I was disconnected.

Nicki and I had cleared up our trust issues. It no longer mattered to me what had happened. She remained completely committed to the job at hand of trying to move the business forward, while I was being torn in so many different directions. In reality, had she not been there, we would have closed down. It was impossible for me to go back to that position. Nicki was better at managing the clients than I ever was. I also no longer had the desire, the focus, or the confidence. I was a different woman from the person who started Wizbot.

I finally sold the press in August 2011. I waited too long. I was desperate and was unable to negotiate; I had to take what they offered. I remember sitting with Donna and questioning why I always make these decisions too late. If I had taken that offer a year ago, Wizbot would have been two hundred thousand dollars ahead. She just shook her head and said, "Wendy, you weren't ready to let it go." Ya, that seemed to be the story of my life, I could always make the right decision when it was too late. With the little bit of money left from the sale I was able to pay for the other presses to be moved allowing us to downsize again. We were now under ten thousand square feet and I had managed to cut our rent in half. Unfortunately, I also had to lay Harry off. I hated it. Harry had been one of our pressmen for over ten years. He was a good man. He was from Newfoundland, and I always said the world needed more "Newfies." They have more heart, more perspective, more life in them.

The summer came and went. The legal world was like nothing I had ever experienced. It moves lightening fast to get you hooked, and then slows down to a turtle's pace while your money is siphoned away. We finally had a Discovery date in September. The day arrived and then got cancelled while I was sitting in the room waiting for it to begin. Some technicality had arisen and Sam now threatened to claim bankruptcy. I was beside myself with anger. He was guilty as sin and I wanted my day in court. It was a year and a half into the process and I had accrued almost thirty thousand in legal costs. Wizbot was teetering on the edge, my life was in shambles and I honestly believed all of this was because Sam felt entitled to my business.

The truth is I could now write a book on how broken and costly our legal system is. My battle, and all of the wasteful and unethical things that took place, are probably a common occurrence. I am not talking about my lawyer Herb, who is a very generous and decent man. The rest, though, was beyond comprehension. I have over a thousand pieces of paper from this journey, but I am going to leave many of the events out of this story. They serve no purpose now.

This story is about late October 2011. I am laying on the white couch, the place where you were most likely to find me. It became my retreat and my refuge. You see, over the course of all of this, I never faced what was really happening. I was telling Dan that everything would work out and I believed that it would. But, I had also promised him that we would not lose the house. The line of credit had gotten too high and the math no longer worked. It happens when you do not have an income, are selling RRSPs to cover living expenses, and paying both a mortgage and huge line of credit interest.

Once again, I waited too long to face the truth. We needed to put the house up for sale, but now there was no time. I had nothing left in me physically or emotionally to clean it up, to get it presentable, yet the need to sell was now. I had thrown so much money into Wizbot to cover payroll and to keep it alive. We were so far into it, I could not see how to stop. Even if I shut Wizbot down, what would I do? How would I support our life? If every receivable came in and all the equipment was sold, by the time the employees were compensated there would be nothing left.

I needed someone else to take the reigns from me, someone else to drive this coach that was running down the hill out of control. I no longer had the strength or the capabilities. I just held on and hoped. I had no idea what else to do; I did not know how to ask or even whom to ask. I didn't know how to let go.

There was a letter in the mailbox, it was there the next day. It was from a woman named Jodi, same name as our daughter. Her family was looking to buy a house in our neighbourhood. If we were interested in selling she asked that we contact her. It was a gift; it was an answer to my prayers. Just like in my youth, help arrived unexpectedly when the need was greatest. It was the first sign in over a year that things might be turning around.

We met with them, and it happened quickly. We did not barter much on price. They wanted to build their dream home on our lot, so our house was going to be a tear down. I focused in on the three things I wanted the most: a fair price, a quick close, and money in the bank as soon as possible. To meet those goals I came up with the idea we would sell with an immediate closing. Then we would rent our house back from them for a year, while they made their design plans.

We had the money in the bank by December, paid off all of our personal debts, and now had a year to focus on what we would do for living arrangements. We hoped it would be a home in the same area. We had enough money to purchase a small home, but until the business could pay us a salary, we could not make any plans.

I used to love Christmas. I loved wishing everyone good cheer, and I especially loved buying gifts for the customers and employees. Over the last couple of years it had became more difficult, but now it was impossible. Now Christmas was the most stressful, frustrating time of the year. Not only did I have no money for gifts, closing down shop and the annual downturn in business were crushing. It was not a matter of if we would lose money; it was a matter of how much.

I had looked forward to 2012 and the idea of a new year, just the symbolism that perhaps something new and fresh would bring good things. The lawyers office was working on a motion to possibly take Sam's lawyer to task over the last discovery we finally had last October 30. The number of refusals Jim Lion had used was beyond anything Herb had ever seen in his many years of practicing law. It was so bad and belligerent that Herb had shut it down. He closed his note book and said he would not continue. It was an awful day and a waste of my money. I was tired of the games and any judgment against Jim Lion would at least bring me some satisfaction.

People were wondering how I was coping. How did I still manage to joke and stand up everyday? Donna knew what was going on; others knew about the suit but not the rest. I was coping just fine. I stayed to my routine of going to work and driving kids to dance. But when the driving was done, and I was home for the night at 9:30, I would have my wine, always just planning on a couple of glasses. I would catch up on the day's politics in front of the computer. There at night, when the world had gone to bed, I became Golfergirl on political forums, and wailed at the world. My resentments were many.

Those two glasses of wine became a bottle. The world that was once so glorious, the hope and the opportunities and the freedom – they were all just a lie. I was stuck, frozen, completely detached from anything I once was.

Chapter 10

Soulless

*Thank you for this meal we are about to receive,
may we not take for granted our good fortune,
but rather find gratitude in our hearts that
we are not living in hunger.*

*Thank you for the love of family,
may we not take for granted the warmth
and security we derive from this bond.*

*Thank you for this life, may we not squander the
gifts we have been given, but rather embrace them.
May we come to the realization that free will has
been endowed to all humanity and when
we respect each other's freedom,
we will finally understand
the meaning of peace on earth.*

It was Friday May 11, 2012. Mom's distended stomach was now awkwardly large and we were finally meeting the surgeon. She had waited six weeks for a CT scan, far too long in hindsight. I met Mom and David at the cancer centre in Hamilton. Jodie had a dance competition about an hour away in St. Catharines that weekend. She was dancing in the afternoon, so my brother Greg took her and my niece Alanna, Greg's youngest daughter. I planned on heading to the competition after Mom's appointment.

David, Mom and I went to reception, where they sent Mom off for some blood work. This all started with an upset stomach the morning after Jodie's dance showcase, in late February. Now here we were at a cancer hospital. We knew the meeting was not going to be an easy one, cancer had touched too many lives in our family. It was a fact of life for us: a given, not a shock. While Mom was getting her blood work done, I went outside to check my messages. The name on the email stood out immediately, it was from the lawyer's office. I knew I should not read it, this was not the time, but I did. I had to. It was a notice that Sam had filed for bankruptcy. This was terrible news, meaning my case against him was stayed. If he went into bankruptcy, my claim would be dropped. Everything I had been fighting for: my day in court, my restitution, all would disappear down the rabbit hole. Two years of this hell had been for nothing. How could he? He had a house, a business, money?

The lawyer's office called me. They informed me that Sam and his wife had filed for separation, and on that basis, he was giving her everything, paying the highest support, and offering the house at the end. I could not listen anymore. It was all a scam. It made me sick, made me ill. At this moment however, I had no choice but to let it go. It was not my priority.

We went up to the Doctor's office, where Mom was taken into an examination room. Once the exam was finished, David and I were invited in. Her stomach was huge and she needed surgery right away, but the earliest he could operate was June 11th, a month away! There was nothing the surgeon could do; there was no other time available. He believed she had ovarian cancer or it could be in the bowels. They scheduled a biopsy for May 30th to determine the exact diagnosis. The 30th would be Mom's 73rd birthday. I tried to take notes, keep my mind clear and ask questions. I knew we were discussing cancer, yet I was not feeling any fear. It was matter of fact: They would operate, and she would go home and recover. Just like Dan did, just like my niece and nephew, just like all the women I knew with breast cancer.

On top of everything else it was Mother's Day weekend and this was the last dance competition of the season for Jodie. It was Shine Dance, one of my favourites. Most years there was nothing I wanted more for Mother's Day than the bond of being at a dance competition with my daughter. There is nothing better than watching your child do something they love. I loved witnessing her run around with her pack: the great group of girls she dances with. Nothing matches watching her prepare, her range of emotions, getting her head in the right place to dance, and her success in finding the right combination of confidence, fear, humility, and gratitude. The desire to compete is intense, to dig deep and find the better you. Okay those are her mother's feelings, not sure what is going on in her head, but I am sure it is some of those things.

This year was different. I needed this escape, but it was not about me the mother. It was about me the daughter. Even though I was in complete denial that anything bad would happen to Mom, there was no escaping that she had cancer and was in for a long battle.

That Friday was a surreal day. I was on the phone for a good chunk of the way to the competition. Dan and I had bought a plaquing and laminating business, it was closing at the end of May and we had only three weeks to pull it off. This had been my insane idea: to purchase a floundering business in the hopes we could rebuild it, as a back up plan, in case Wizbot failed. It would be a company for Dan to build on his own. It seemed kind of brilliant at the time: spend some of the house money on something we could build on, before the money ran out. A business without employees. It would have none of those responsibilities and regulations that were now dragging me down, weighing so heavily on my shoulders. It was insanity, I still had full time work and headaches at Wizbot, why did I do this?

I got to the competition with little time to spare. I don't remember what dances she had that day, except for her tap duet. It was a Michael Jackson number: *Black and White*. Jodie and her partner wore leather jackets and black, gangster hats. I will never forget that accessory because Jodie could not find her hat. It must have been left in my brother's car, and he had gone back to Burlington. The hats were an integral part of the number. For all of the important life moments that day, I was panicking and breaking down over her hat. I knew she was stressing over letting her partner down, worried the teachers were going to be upset. She was trying to take responsibility, while at the same time knowing that this day was different. It was the first time I had not been there with her to prepare.

It was strange how that stupid hat affected me. I wanted to cry; I lost my composure. I would not let myself dwell on my mother's cancer. I would not allow myself to even consider the possibility she might not live. I would not stress over Sam's bankruptcy, that would be my challenge, another chess move I would have to make. The business deal would get done; I had until May 30th. In my crazy world that was plenty of time. The hat however, that was traumatic. I had no control and I could not fix it. It became the crux of my despair. I was a crazy lady breaking down over a missing hat for a three minute dance.

The next night we celebrated Mother's Day at the Keg, a restaurant near the competition. We were a large party. Cherin was in the area for a swim meet that her youngest Jaqueline was competing in. They joined Greg, his youngest Alanna, his fiancee Sandy, Dan, Jodie and myself and of course my Mom and David for dinner. It was a beautiful night. The waiter teased the girls about knowing Justin Bieber. Jackie, a whole 80 pounds soaking wet, tried to make a deal that if she ate an entire rack of ribs, would he get her tickets to his concert. My Mom, although not well, never let it show. She was glowing, soaking in the atmosphere, and enjoying the occasion of having all three of her children together. It was truly a night where everyone appreciated the good fortune of having a close family. It was also our last supper together. I wish all of the grandchildren could have been there. I wish I had known. As I look back at the pictures of Mom from that night, I now see how ill she really was.

Sunday, May 27, I drove visit Mom in Niagara Falls where she lived. She wanted us to walk to Tim Hortons, just the right distance for her and her distended stomach. Her illness seemed all the more unfair because my mother had always taken care of herself, eaten healthy foods, nothing in excess, went to the gym two to four times a week, and walked daily. We ordered something light and sat down. The place was not very busy, so we could talk without being overheard. Mom starting going through a list of her possessions, naming off three items she wanted to make sure her children would receive. I did not like the conversation; I could not believe we were having this conversation, but I listened, I thought I should let Mom have her say. Then I thanked her and said we would not need to worry about any of it, because it was crazy talk. Mom was too fit to be dying anytime soon.

May 29th was Jodie's 13th birthday. I had nothing special prepared, in keeping with the story of my life: always flying by the seat of my pants, never organized, just getting things done. The business deal was closing the next day, I had issues with the paper work around both setting up the corporation and the operating name. The bank account hinged on the paperwork. The lawyers on the other end were making some difficult demands at the last hour. I had finally settled the negotiations with the landlord, but everything else was a never ending list of documents to complete and follow up phone calls to make. I was driving back from Mississauga when I got the call from Dan. David had called in a panic, Mom had gone to emergency in Niagara Falls in a lot of pain. He did not know what hospital.

I just started driving to Niagara Falls, pulling over half way to get the address of the hospital. Mom was on a stretcher in the hallway. One of many stretchers in the hallway of an overloaded emergency department. She was in pain but not complaining, just lying there as Mom would, telling herself to be patient and strong. Her stomach was huge; she looked like she was going to give birth to twins. How could this be happening so fast? We were there for hours. They gave her something for the pain and left us waiting for a plan, for an answer.

Mom needed surgery right away, but no one yet knew for sure what cancer they were dealing with. She had her biopsy scheduled for the next morning at the cancer centre in Hamilton, they were the specialists. It was all we could think about. We needed to get her there. A choice had to be made: she could go to that appointment the next day, or they start devising a plan at the hospital in Niagara Falls. Well, past history told us that we wanted the experts. Mom's sister Donna had died from cancer in her 50s, after deciding to go with the local hospital, instead of the specialist's, in Toronto. Mom's grandchildren Martin and Avalon had experienced great results with specialists. Mom made the decision to wait for the biopsy. For some reason, we were all zeroed in on that test. We were stuck on the plan, we could not see that the moment had called for a new thought process.

I arranged for patient transport to take Mom to Hamilton early the next morning. It was a 6:30 am pick up on her birthday. I had contacted my sister and she was making the five hour drive in from Brockville. I sat with Mom while we waited at the cancer centre. When we finally went in, they were surprised she had left the hospital in the Falls, as she was in serious need of surgery. They did the procedure, then moved us to another wing where they did a battery of tests and prepared her for the unknown. Unfortunately, the unknown was that they had no beds. Many caring people met with her and all agreed she was in immediate need, but they had no beds. They sent her home with instructions on when to call an ambulance. The hope was she would have a bed the next day.

I had the business deal to close, so Cherin took over while I went back to Burlington to take care of the banking and contracts. Cherin was the youngest: my annoying little sister. But she grew up to be the wisest, the one who knew what really mattered in life: Love and family. She took Mom and David back to the Falls, comforted and cared for them.

Thursday the 31st of May, Cherin brought Mom back to the cancer centre. They entered through emergency, so they had to take her in. They still lacked beds, but this time they set up a temporary room in the visitor's lounge on the floor where she should have been placed. It was actually the nicest room on the floor with plenty of space for us all to gather around Mom. By this time both Greg and I were just doing the bare minimum on our respective businesses, wanting to stay at the hospital with Cherin, our mother and David. Beautiful David, twelve years Mom's senior and refusing to leave her side for anything. He loved her, as he loved life itself. Oh, to witness that type of love. I had seen it before when Cherin's first son Martin was battling leukemia, at the age of four. Cherin lived by his side in a hospital room for a month. She would not even leave the hospital for a lunch break. She would stay and fight with him, telling him he had super heroes in his body fighting off the bad guys.

They explained to us on Thursday night, that although Mom needed surgery, she had fluid build up on her lungs. They had to take care of that first. They finally got her a bed and prepared a plan, or at least moved towards getting her ready for surgery.

And so the weekend came and went. Now it was Monday June 4, Cherin's birthday. The most important beautiful women in my life, all have their birthdays within a week of each other. This was always time for our family to gather in celebration of the birthdays of my mother, my sister and my daughter. Today however was no celebration. The surgeon sent the intern to inform us that her lungs were clear but no surgery was yet scheduled. David got angry, I had never seen David so angry. Why were they not doing something? The doctor explained that they still needed the results of the biopsy to fully understand Mom's case. They had to know what they were dealing with. The perfect plan. They wanted the perfect plan, but while they waited for that, they were losing their patient. Our mother was lying in pain; she could hardly swallow. Everything was upsetting her stomach and -her system was backing up. A diet of morphine and Gravol gave her no comfort what-so-ever. We took turns passing her ice chips and wiping her forehead with a cool cloth. Cherin was there, always there.

Wednesday June 6 came. There was talk that the surgery might happen soon, perhaps on Thursday. They changed Mom's medications. When I arrived that afternoon, she was looking better than she had for days. A little bit of pain and torture had been removed, and she had a little life in her eyes. She was feeling a little better, and even laughed. It made us feel good to think she might have more strength for the surgery.

Cherin and David had been there all day, so they left for a rest on a happier note. Greg and Sandy said their goodbyes, and then I settled in for some evening time with Mom. Her new medication arrived. I had watched the nurses at shift change and listened as they discussed the order in which it must be administered. The new nurse went about her job. I wondered, then second guessed myself.

It happened quickly, the turn in Mom's condition. Emergency lights and beepers went off and I was whisked out of the room, while a variety of personnel arrived with different equipment. I watched from the hallway as they got her vital signs back under control: her breathing. It was three years ago and I do not remember the medical terms used. My intuition was screaming at me, I knew by the hushed tones and discussions, my heart was aching for everyone in that room. I don't remember much else other than my decision. I sat with Mom for a couple of hours afterwards. It was now ten or eleven. There had been so many late nights, so many emotions, and I was feeling terrible about not being home at night with Jodie. Terrible about leaving the new business, and terrible about not being at Wizbot. Completely guilt ridden on every front. I was not just tired, I was completely drained. The doctor said something about the possibility of a tube, I didn't know what that was, like the lien on the car and 35mm vs IMAX. I didn't say I do not understand, please explain this to me. I leaned over, kissed my Mom on the forehead, and reassured her that it would be okay. She looked at me and said, "Will it really?" Like a child asking me for reassurance. I said yes, so certain was I that it would. When the male nurse saw me at the elevator, he asked if I was going home. I said yes. There was something in his voice that made me stop and turn back, but then I changed my mind and returned to the elevator. I was tired and needed to be home. I needed my strength for the coming surgery.

Mom was very clear that she did not want to be kept on life support. The only way she wanted to live was in full mind and body. I guess I should have known, should have listened to that voice in my head, the one that said – "Stay Wendy, call your sister and brother and David. Hold her hand and stay." The anxiety owned me all night, I could not push it aside. Was it doubt and fear or was it intuition?

Cherin called me and said I needed to come right away. It was Thursday afternoon and we had been in touch throughout the day. Mom had been put on life support in the early hours. They had asked her if she wanted anyone to call us, and she had said no. It would be just like Mom to not want to bother anyone, either that or she had made her decision and did not want us to change it.

Mom was now in a different wing of the hospital. I had to pass a chapel to get there; the waiting area was now a grieving room. I knew why I was coming. I was not ready. Cherin and David had been there all day, and had time to digest and to gather information. They were where I should have been. I have never felt so helpless and hopeless in all of my life. Greg was there, our strong and loving brother, but even he could not hide the pain. It was June 7, 2012, four days before the originally scheduled surgery. My mother should have had that surgery. There was nothing right about watching her last breath. It never should have been that way.

The diagnosis was Sarcoma, a cancer in the muscles. I could go on about all of the things that were wrong about our mother's death: I could talk about the insanity of fighting the hospital for an autopsy that Cherin was willing to pay for. Why, why were they trying to talk us out of this? The fact that the surgery should have happened weeks before. The intense anger I had towards that surgeon who would not operate, who would not allow her the chance to battle for her life on the operating table. The six week wait for a CT scan, why so long with a distended stomach? The possibility of an error in the administration of medicine. An autopsy report that when it did come back almost a year later, our brown eyed mother now had blue eyes. But really, what does it matter now, that is not where this story goes.

This story goes to a family grieving back home, back at Dan's and my home. Dan had come outside where we were all sitting in the back yard. He asked what time Mom had passed, and we all agreed it was around 4:45. He asked me to come in the house and he pointed to the old clock that had come from Mom's Dad. It had stopped working at 4:45.

Flowers were delivered to our house that evening. They were from my friend Michele who did not know our mother: African violets, beautiful blossoming purple. I burst into tears. It was hard for me to fathom. Mom always had purple African Violets in her home.

It was not long after my Mom passed, I think it was July, when Donna was diagnosed with breast cancer. We were in shock. Life just kept getting uglier. I didn't know how I was going to make it through without having Donna at work, and not just because of the amazing work she did. She was my rock; she held me together. We could laugh and joke to take away the insane pressure of trying to keep the doors open. Why her? She had been through enough, as well. What was happening to the world around me? Why were all of the good people suffering?

And so began my year of mourning, and anger and self-hate. I went to places in my soul I had never been before. I had never known what it was like to be so hopeless and helpless. Everything that mattered to me was gone, except Jodie. She was the only thing that gave me any joy in life, any purpose. I was not going to lay that on her; I was not going to lean on her. But the days began to just roll by as I fled more frequently to a dream world on the white couch: frozen. I lost my ability to make decisions and my energy to do simple tasks. My only joy was watching Jodie dance.

We will all endure a time of grieving at some point in our lives. They say the first year is incredibly hard, and it was. But for me it was more than that. I couldn't control myself. Every day for months on end, the tears came. No matter how hard I tried not to think about it. All it took was just a word, a thought, or a date and I was broken. Jodie's dance competitions were especially hard, Mom would always be there, but now she was not.

I had my last drink October 21st, 2012. It was the only good thing about that year. I did it for Jodie, or at least so Jodie could have a mother she could count on. I had hit an emotional rock bottom; I realized that I was no longer fooling my thirteen year old. I had spent so many years teaching her life was awesome and we have control over our lives and feelings, yet here I was broken and out of control. I wish I could remember where I got the strength. I think I was just trying to make myself more miserable. I wasn't thinking about tomorrow. I was thinking about how much I hated myself, and I could not imagine living a life where my daughter saw me the same way.

The year 2012 rolled by. Now there were two businesses: One not making money, and the other losing money. The lawsuit was gone leaving me fighting Sam's bankruptcy. There was no way I was letting him off the hook that easy. You don't screw someone's life up, run away when you have had enough, and then hide behind a nine month bankruptcy.

It seems there are a thousand companies out there if you want to go into bankruptcy, but try finding one that will help you fight against a bankruptcy claim. Nobody cares. Bankruptcies are always against those supposedly big, evil, heartless corporations. Whatever happened to the shame in being bankrupt? For my Dad it was seven years of shame. Now it is only nine months and they make it sound like a victimless crime.

I finally found a great firm to handle my case. Sam's separation agreement and lack of full disclosure appeared to be a fraudulent transaction. It also appeared to me that he was claiming bankruptcy on two corporate credit cards. How on earth do you file bankruptcy on a debt that is not your own! How many battles did I have to fight? Had the whole world gone corrupt?

This lawyer was amazing and I was looking forward to working with him. But as my life went, at the 11th hour when the motion was set to go, Sam's Dad Norm used his connections to get to the partners in the firm. My new lawyer informed me that he had to drop me as a client. How do you drop a client at this stage in the game? This was the end of November, and I had to have this dealt with before February 4. I had to start all over with another firm and explain the whole case. All I had was two months and one of them was December. Who works in December at Christmas time?

I was living life by just putting one foot in front of the other. That is how I got up and through every day, I told myself to just put one foot in front of the other. Full of anger and self-hate, I was physically drained and emotionally filled with the poison I had been feeding myself: the government, the legal system, the health care system. People. People were all mean and cruel and ignorant. No one had principles. That is what my new lawyers in bankruptcy told me, "Wendy if you are doing this for principle, then you will be sorely disappointed."

I am a fighter, not a violent person, not a hate-filled person, just a stubborn woman who cannot stand to lose. It's what makes me a survivor; it's in my DNA. Unfortunately sometimes our strengths are also our weaknesses. What keeps me standing, also clouds my judgement. These raw nerves, this passion-filled heart clung to this false purpose and blinded me. Everyone around me was starting to cave, starting to suggest that maybe I should just let it go. How could I, I am not a quitter. I knew I had taken this further than anyone expected. I knew I was wasting money I did not have to spend, but I could not stop. The more I saw the underbelly of this cruel world, the more I felt I was being asked to soldier on.

2013 arrived. I love the number 13, and so I was hopeful that our Wizbot world would change. I tried to be optimistic, to look for positive signs, and to believe that we would get a break or two. Maybe we would get something back in return, for our hard work and struggles.

Of course it didn't change. Wizbot stayed the course of losing money, except now I had the weight of the second business. I also promised to find us a new home and pack up the ten years of mind-boggling stuff we had collected. In Dan's eyes, I had done this to the family. He wanted nothing to do with the move; it was my problem. I saw where he was coming from, and understood his hurt and sense of helplessness. I also realized that the two of us had passed the point of finding a middle ground. I came to resent him. Oh sure, I would go through stages of thinking about fixing things, but only halfheartedly. The second business was yet another of my ideas that had only complicated our life. The intention was good; it was so he had something, some work that would fill him, and that he could call his own.

In March we were told the house was coming down in July. We had to be out by the end of June. We had to commit to a date as they were counting on our rent money. I was so incensed that there was no wiggle room past June. It was the one month I had asked that we not have to move. There had been no time for me to find a place yet. Having a dog and our goal to stay in the school boundaries complicated the search. I had promised Jodie we would stay in the area. After all of my struggles in my youth changing schools, there was no way I would let Jodie down on this one.

It was April and my search was not going well. Just when I thought I may have to act a little unscrupulously with the school boundaries, I received a gift. I had gone home for lunch, something I rarely did, when I saw the "For Rent" sign that had just been posted. It was a house in the area. I knew I had to act fast so I called right away. I agreed to the rent although it was much higher than I wanted to pay. I negotiated possession for the middle of May at no cost, so I could clean and move in slowly.

It should have been plenty of time and an easy move but it wasn't. May and June were our busiest months at Wizbot. Work was crazy busy, and I had no drive or energy. Packing and cleaning were more than I could handle. I was so grateful for my brother helping Dan physically move some things. My ex-sister-in-law Karen, helped me clean the new place.

Jodie kept me standing. Her grade eight grad and dance recital were the end of June. Everything was happening at once. The movers came the day of her grad and the weekend of her recital followed. It was crazy for her trying to get ready with the house in such disarray, but she kept a positive happy attitude. There was still so much garbage and junk to deal with at the old house. We were never really ready, and all I heard as I was cleaning out our old home that we never wanted to leave, was how terrible the new rental was.

I was forced to sign a new lease at Wizbot. It was 30 pages of legal jargon, in stark contrast to the the old days when it was just one. The lawyers were now running the world and there was nothing I could do to fight it. The long and short, my rent expenses, taxes and maintenance were going up. A twenty percent increase and there was nothing I could do about it. Moving my equipment would cost me thousands of dollars I did not have. On top of everything, our utilities were skyrocketing thanks to government policy. I was bitterly convinced that there was an agenda to shut down manufacturing in Ontario. Actually everything was skyrocketing in price, and every time I thought we were making progress, we got pulled backwards.

I tried to get new business, but to no avail. I used to land everything, now I couldn't land a blood starved mosquito. I knew it was me, but I couldn't find what I needed in my heart to make a sale. I was lost and broken. All I could do was just go through the motions of getting up, going to work and trying not to get too miserable.

In late August of 2013 my friend Michele, a fellow dance Mom held a surprise fiftieth birthday party for me. I was deeply moved by the gesture, and all of the people who made a point of attending. But it was, as I refer to her now, dead Wendy that had shown up.

Michele's back yard was filled with everyone who was dear to me. She even invited my golf girlfriends, my BBG. There was music and alcohol. I was ten months sober at the time, nobody knew that I was trying to quit drinking for good. I was always just saying no thank you and not tonight. I wanted a drink, I wanted to drink up my numbness and let it all out. I was feeling desperate to escape. Somehow I stayed strong. I think it was having Jodie and all of her beautiful dance friends there. That was the highlight for me. For all of the misery I was feeling, those girls reminded me of hope and possibilities. They reminded me of who I used to be, fun and full of life.

Laura came up to me to say good-bye, I had expected smiles yet there were tears. She gave me a hug and said I love you but it breaks my heart that you let one man change you. Don't let one man change you. And with that she and my BBGs left the party. I looked around the yard to see who remained at my surprise 50th. It was all new friends: the Dance moms and their teenage daughters. It was surreal to see my two worlds collide and I realized this was the part of the movie where the Warner Brothers logo comes and says, "The End." Without a doubt I realized a part of my life had ended. Despite all of the want in the world, I could not jump back into that circle of friends, Laura was right. I had changed, but it was not one man who had changed me.

Life brought me to where I then stood. I didn't know if it was the right place; it was certainly not a joyous place. It was not carefree, simple, or filled with abundance. The rose-coloured glasses were gone. I didn't expect I would find them again, at least not the pair that had made me naïve to the world around me. Was it an awakening or the natural process of life? Was I somewhere I would have eventually reached over time, or was it shaken out of me? The search for truth was still my guiding light. It was not like I had not been looking, yet there I stood and nothing looked or felt as it had three and a half years before.

I was not walking around with a sour puss face and saying poor me. But I was dead inside and every attempt at smiling and humour was a motion without light. I was tired and overwhelmed. I did my best impression of a woman genuinely happy. I was grateful but I could not release the misery or find joy anywhere.

Chapter 11

The Intervention

Today I heard the voice of fear,
it was whispering to me.
What If? What if this happened?

So I changed fear's words to What Is.

What is in front of me at this moment is all I know.
I will deal with what if, should what if arise.
But for now there is only what is.

So I accepted what is and moved on,
and looked over my shoulder for fear,
and there in the new light I saw
it was serenity that now had appeared.

If you had a moment in time, a day, a thought or a series of thoughts that came to you all at once, that drastically and instantly changed your outlook on life, changed your thinking, the way you felt, what would you call it? If that moment was surreal, but you are logical and rational, yet the power of the images and the feelings were greater than your conscious mind, what would you call it? For the sake of no better explanation, I call it my intervention. Whether it was subconscious or a matter of my own blinders falling off, whether it was my mother reaching out to me from heaven or God saving me, it was the most powerful, inexplicable, incomprehensible moment of my life.

To call it divine would make it of God or from God. An intervention is something that changes your direction, your path. It interferes with what you are doing, or in this case, where I was going. What created the intervention or what intervened can be explained – I am sure – by psychologists or therapists. In fact upon reading this book, I am sure they will have many neat and tidy little boxes, to put me in, and labels to attach. I have my own labels. It is possible I am bat shit crazy, mildly insane or suffering from a mid-life crisis extraordinaire. Either way, I am okay with whatever people choose to believe, as I have regained my inner peace and happiness from the events of that day. Believing it was divine intervention makes me content in the knowledge that I am exactly where I am meant to be right now. It gives me the strength and confidence to write this book, and to know I am fulfilling my contract with myself and my higher power. If I am bat shit crazy, well what a great opportunity for the analysts to view the inner workings of a broken mind.

I am in my office at my desk having lunch, it is a salad. I was fooling myself yet again that I might try to start eating healthier.

I was thinking about the gala I had attended the night before. It was a beautiful evening, 600 plus people, all trying to make a difference. We had all been touched by the story of Elisa, and moved by the incredible courage and conviction of her family. The Sanfilippo Foundation was started 15 years ago by the Lintons. Their third child Elisa was diagnosed with Sanfilippo Syndrome. A rare and ugly disease that involves a missing enzyme, the absence of which reverses the mental capacity and leaves the child with a life expectancy of about 16 years.

There they were: One family and over three million dollars raised. Could you imagine going to the hospital and being told your four year old daughter has this terrible disease, and even worse, imagine being told that nothing could be done. There is no research, no formal treatment, no care or in essence, no hope. It was the thought of no hope that got me. I have seen cancer visit my family on numerous occasions. For the adults the battle was rarely won, but for the children, my niece and nephew, they were given "buts." Yes this is a terrible disease and it can take their lives, "but," we have new technology, new procedures, new drugs. They were given hope and 18 years later, you would never know they had battled cancer.

So Elisa and the Lintons are my most important charity. Had it not been for the people that supported cancer research years ago, my niece, Avalon and my nephew, Martin, would not be where they are today: two awesome, solid, wonderful, loving young adults. Those people who gave to cancer research years ago made a difference in their lives.

So, six hundred of us were at the gala the night before my intervention trying to make a difference. This night in particular, even more so than in the past, I felt the connection and love. This was a family so firm and committed to their faith; they were everything good about church and community. No matter how hard the battle or how long, they never gave up hope. They never laid down and said this journey is too much. They soldiered on for their little girl, and all the children like her, that they may have a breakthrough, a "but" in their lifetime.

I attended the gala with Cindy, my "date" for 15 years. It was not Dan's thing and Cindy was more fun on these occasions, anyway. In the past my friend Jim came and acted as our escort. Jim and I went back years to the old Sony Music days. We were just kids then, having a ball working at a record company thinking we had it made. Jim and I played mixed baseball. He played short stop and I stood at second where I watched him make play after play on his side and my side of the bag. What can I say? He could cover more ground in one step then I could in four. He ran the football pool, and I donated money to his football pool. We bet on and watched all sorts of sports together. We were good friends and he was as cute as a button. Okay more like tall and incredibly attractive, inside and out. He is the perfect man and a very good friend.

Jim moved to Texas with his wife Sue and their two adorable little girls. Going to the gala was still a highlight of sorts, but not having Jim to play escort meant the evening was never quite the same.

But this night was different. Unbeknownst to me, but known to Cindy and the Lintons, Jim had booked a business trip around the gala. He was going to be in Toronto and they all thought it would be fun to surprise me. It worked. I was so happy to see Jim and so touched that they would keep it a secret. I loved Jim, not in a romantic way, he was a friend: a solid guy and a part of my history, my young days, my adventure days.

And so it was from that night that my gratitude blossomed. The Lintons announced that they were ready to start clinical trials. That the money raised had made a difference; there was hope after 16 years. It was uplifting and the spirit of good will in the room was palpable.

Jim being there, playing our escort and taking care of everyone. Cindy, working the room and making us laugh. She is as solid of a friend as you could ever ask for, filled with kindness and full of mischief. I had much to be grateful for and on that particular night, for the first time in what seemed like eternity, the world did not look so damn ugly to me.

So on April 24, 2014, sitting in my office eating lunch, I thought of Jim and his surprise attendance the previous night. He was tall, handsome and just so kind, caring and wonderful around all people – all people, from all walks of life, in all shapes and sizes. Never judging, just making people feel good, making them laugh, making them feel special. Our friendship was exactly that: a friendship. This does not stop me from trying to imagine what a different relationship would be like, not with Jim, but with someone like him. Why am I doing that? I have Dan. We have been together for 24 years, but we are miserable; we are toxic. We are that couple in the restaurant staring at the walls with nothing to say. We are broken and empty, yet we continue on, both thinking one day we will fix what is broken. How long has it been like that: five years, 10 years, maybe 15?

I remember a moment early in my relationship with Dan. He was teaching me how to play squash and the lesson started with a verbal explanation. He was showing me how to hold the racquet, how to swing the racquet, and how to transfer my weight. We started to play. He would stop me and show me what I was doing wrong and hit the ball again. I would attempt to return it. He would stop and correct me again. It went like this for a while, until the last time he stopped me I could no longer help myself and it just came out, "I just want to hit the fucking ball."

I shocked myself and him, but I just wanted to swing that racquet. I wanted to try it on my own, to learn from doing not from being told. I wanted him to give me the basics, but the rest was for me to learn and do on my terms. That was Dan and I: Him trying to teach me, trying to impart his wisdom on me and me feeling the weight of him trying to control, making me feel little.

There are so many levels to love someone, parents, children, brother and sister, great friends, good samaritans, I thought I knew them all; I thought I loved Dan. If you had never known any differently you assume that what you know is love. So it was for me. How do I fix this love? How do we stop arguing? How do I get back on track so I want to go home instead of avoiding it? I live wondering if we can even be civil each day. How did it get to this? I had to try to be kinder. I had to try to be more loving, and more sensitive to his needs. I had to find it inside me to want to, that is what made fixing things such a difficult task. I had to want to find the love we once had, I had to try to remember what that love looked like, I had to know what love was. I hated myself. I did not know what love was anymore; I was incapable of love, I used to think I had a cup overflowing with love, not now. Now I was a stone. I felt nothing; I was living in emptiness. My mind, my heart and my body, were completely devoid of life. I was desolate.

I did not have the desire or energy to think about my relationship with Dan. It was what it was. Like everything else in life, you just go forward, soldier on, put on a brave face and hope things get better.

A face, an image came into my thoughts. It did not belong and it actually made me laugh. Instinctively I thought, really, you have to be kidding! It was here that I broke away from my standard protocol. At any other time, on any other given day, I would have dismissed that image and gone back to my conscious self. I am not one to indulge in fantasy, if it takes me down a path that is outside my comfort zone. That is how I stay grounded, how I stay on track, how I try to remain true to my principles? Morals? Whatever. It is just what I have always done. If it is not a comfortable thought and holds no intellectual value, I banish it. But this day I did not. This day, this moment, I gave it life. I opened my eyes and faced it, I literally sat stunned; I was blown away, shocked, confused and completely hypnotized. I could not let this go. I could not look away. It stopped being an image and became a feeling.

Joy, it was joy that I just felt. Why? I could not believe the rush of life that just swept over me. I wanted to cry; I wanted to hug the world for I just felt something. I had just became human for the first time in an eternity. The realization of what it meant to be alive, to feel something other than wounded. Could I again feel excited, carnal, something/anything other than the emptiness that had held me, owned me, and had become me?

It was a moment, nothing short of an intervention. Divine? Maybe?

Yet there was nothing divine in what I just felt, or was there? For years now I just felt dead; I was empty. There was no way in my drained and grieving state that I could have created that moment: that realization that life and all its glory had just been breathed back into my soul. A second chance or a vision? I cry as I write this. I was lost for so long and, out of nowhere this path opened up: this way out, this way forward. Was it always there and I was too blind to see it? Was my mind so mired in anger and defeat? Hope had come calling and I was not going to let it go.

Slowly it starts, I know that. You lose a little bit each day, so small that you do not notice, until over time the light has gone out and you get used to living in darkness. Everything I used to love doing had no appeal to me. I could not find joy in anything. Sure I could function: I could say that life was awesome, I could tell a joke, I could socialize, but it was never with anything except a sense of duty. My friends knew it. My sister knew it. I could hear them say, "You are not happy, you are not the same." They were of course right, and I knew it. Every day I tried to talk myself into fixing it, like you could just say, " Today I will be better" and magically heal. But you cannot. This I know from the bottom of my heart, actually from rock bottom I know this. First I had to remember what joy and happiness looked like. I had to want it, to realize I needed it, and then from there I could see my way out, my way to finding me again.

The image was the face of someone I knew, and in that brief moment it hit me that I may be in love with them. Yet it was love on a level I had never known before. The complexity was huge. Maybe that is why I indulged it. It was so foreign and unfathomable that my curiosity was piqued. It was someone that I had known for years, but never thought of in this light. Could not have thought of them in this light. I was now ashamed of thinking in this way, or not as I whispered inside, God, is this a gift or is this a test?

The food in my hands lost interest to me. I needed to get out of the office; I needed to go for a drive and sort out this feeling, this moment, this need. Forget the image. What I just felt was passion and joy; I had just been given a breath of life. I focused on that, knowing I was now breathing again. A few hours ago I was dead; now I was alive for the first time in who knows how long. I was no longer treading water. I wanted to live again. Life was no longer something to endure but rather something to embrace. I thought I would never feel this way again. I feared this part of me was gone forever, and all that was left was fulfilling whatever obligations I had. That was it, to toil in misery until such time as I was dismissed. Not a death wish, just a walking dead, waiting to be tapped on the shoulder and relieved of duty.

So, the feeling of gratitude opened my heart. The vision of love or feeling of joy and passion, shook me back to life. It gave me reason, but it was the next thought that put it all together. I needed, more than anything else in the world, to be free. I understood why I had become so lost, why the light had gone out, and why I was living in darkness. I was always struggling with how to fix Dan and I, but it wasn't Dan, it was me. Everything I was living was not me! We argued, we ate dinner in separate rooms, or if it was together we had nothing to say. Our only commonality was the misery we shared. Any words spoken were often accusations or blame. They were attacks on each other, but more often than not, there was just silence. I spent my childhood and most of my life running away from arguments, avoiding unhappy places, and yet here I was living in a perpetual argument.

This day though, as I thought of what needed to be fixed, I realized it just might be that I did not have to fix it, that maybe I could not fix it. It was with that thought I started to feel the weight of the world lifting. I realized I could make a change and go forward, or I could stay where I was and watch the light go out. This time knowing what was happening, this time surrendering my life to the misery, for surely I could not find joy where I was. I had tried and it only managed to weaken me. We were two entirely different people with completely different dreams, different needs and different ways of living. I needed to be free. The thought was overwhelming; it was so powerful it consumed me. I was suffocating and I needed to be free.

I started walking without intention. It was Sunday and I was still completely immersed in my new found thoughts. I needed to get away and find clarity, so I decided to go for a walk. It was a beautiful day and I had energy, something that had escaped me for such a long time. I walked to a little park along the lake, not far away, maybe a kilometre, but for me in my depleted state it was a hike. I sat on a bench and stared at the water. I thought of my mother and felt this was a good place for me to find her, at least her spirit. While I wrestled with what I would do about Dan and I, I saw an older gentleman get up from a nearby bench and head towards me. He walked up to where I sat, turned and faced the lake. I could sense he wanted to talk. He said something about the water, so I asked him if he was once a sailor. "No," he said laughing. I am pretty sure he was in his mid to late 80's; he seemed so gentle. At the same time I could imagine he was quite a strong and handsome man in his younger days. I was also pretty sure I was meant to meet him.

Our conversation was simple and brief. He made a comment about his life passing him by, and I knew this was a melancholy moment for him. I let his words sink in. I asked him what business he had been in. When he told me printing, that he and his brothers ran his father's printing business, I was not the least bit floored by it. I had expected it, for I knew that our meeting was not by chance but by destiny. That was all. There was no great ah-ha moment. No grand words of wisdom that had never been shared before. Just the words that life had passed him by. He was 80-something; I was only 50, not old, just not a child anymore. That brief meeting was something to hold onto when I found myself questioning if I was doing the right thing. Did I want to stay where I was and say life had passed me by?

Over the next few weeks, I started walking more frequently, not just with our dog Scruffles, but on my own with an iPod. I had not listened to music much over the past few years, which was odd considering it had been my passion. I had also lost my appetite. Food had no appeal to me; I would eat only when I felt I needed it. I was more interested in exploring these new feelings, this new life pumping through my body, and hope making its way back into my heart. I felt love, I was alive and I was free. I was not ready to bring these new discoveries to the surface, just happy to know there was hope, and in time I would know what action to take, at least for Dan and I.

The discovery that I was in love with someone, with this person in particular, was a life-altering moment. It wasn't just the new sense of life it gave me, but the way it shaped my view of life and love. The overwhelming feelings of joy and passion were not created by a need to receive but rather a need to give. I wanted to make this person happy, to lift them up, to bring joy and show them the incredible beauty of life. I had never felt this way before:

a need to fill another life with happiness. Making others happy was always something that brought me joy, but this was different. This new feeling was stronger and more powerful. This was my awakening, my breath of life.

To be honest, to find the truth, then all of the facts must be on display, even if they do not agree with the scientists hypothesis; actually, especially if they do not agree. The truth can hurt, the truth can be hard to accept, but the truth, the solution, the answers will never be found if we ignore the facts and cover up that which we find unpleasant.

So it was with my vision. The image, the person was a woman. Seeing her image was so confusing and surprising to me, that my first instinct was to ignore and push aside. Yet in being so confusing and surprising, it piqued my curiosity. I knew it was love, but I felt no physical attraction, at least not on the surface. That was hard for me to understand. How do you love someone like this when you cannot imagine a physical relationship, and when the attraction does not relate to any marker from your previous history? I spent days peeling back layers trying to understand how this attraction evolved. How long had it been there? Was it always there, or just placed there for me that day to save my life?

The idea of a romantic relationship with another woman was not only foreign to me, it was incredibly unsettling. The concept of same gender sex, of even kissing a woman, was almost repulsive to me. It was something I could never comprehend. I was homophobic, not overtly, not something I admonished. I believe in "live and let live," freedom is in my soul. I just could never feel or comprehend same gender attraction. It was like sushi; I had no desire whatsoever to try sushi. So that moment, that day, the

24th of April, I understood love. The feeling was greater, more powerful, more important than issues of straight or gay. This intense love was a gift that I never knew existed.

It was a connection, so deep and powerful, almost like something from another dimension. I used to think the song *Higher Love* was written about world peace, but what I felt at this time was exactly that, some type of higher love. In 50 years of living I had never experienced anything like it.

If nothing else ever came from that moment, I at least had an understanding of what love could look like. In my vision, it was not the physical attraction, but the attraction to the person so deep within my soul. An attraction beyond a normal friendship, an emotional need that had no explanation.

Did I love Dan? Did I ever love Dan? I did as I understood love to be. There had been a physical attraction, a friendship and a sense of caring. A bond existed and there will always be a bond; however there was also an emotional barrier: A difference in visions, and behaviours, and upbringings. It was too hard to ignore. I don't want to walk down that path, the one where we lay blame and try to justify actions. There was much that could be said on both sides, but at the end of the day and from where I sat now, I had only two choices. I could stay and go back into darkness, or end our relationship knowing I might carry the guilt for the rest of my life.

You cannot have your life turned inside out without questioning it, without turning over every stone and looking from every angle. Could I even kiss a woman? Am I gay? Who am I and could I have honestly lived my life for fifty years, without knowing this? At first, in my head, I just called her my soul mate with the wrong plumbing. I was attracted to this person on a level I could not comprehend. What was the reason? Why the attraction? What had brought me here? How many lines would I have to cross, could I cross?

I kept waiting for it to go away, this weird bizarre attraction. I tried to place these feelings elsewhere, but I could not. Not since my teenage years and my love for the "big kid" had I ever felt anything close to this. It was amazing. It was the most powerful combination of emotions I had ever known in my life. I wanted to run from it, and felt I should. I felt I should stop going there and banish it. But I couldn't because it gave me life; it gave me hope.

My heart and mind were open. I did not need to have all of the answers; I knew that time would help me fill in the blanks. I was on a path to discovery, and more importantly, recovery. If nothing else, at least I had a clearer view of love. I thought about my future and what may lay in store for me. I was not about to switch teams, that was out of the question. And yet I was also learning to not close any doors of thought. God, it would appear, had a wicked sense of humour since the image he provided was an antithesis of me.

The conversations in my head with God became frequent. "So okay, you sent me this image of a woman. You want me to learn something. I get that. You are trying to show me something: Maybe some inner truth I have unconsciously covered up for years. Okay, I get that. I'm just not sure I am onside, but considering it beats being the walking dead I can work through it. But why? So now you want to test me! Do you not think I have been tested enough over the last four or five years? Do you not think I have had enough? Why? Why a woman? What purpose does this serve: To shock me, to tease me, to confuse me?

Of course there was nothing I could do. This vision was every line I believed I could never cross. She was an innocent instrument in an unfathomable lesson. There was no possibility of pursuit. I was an attached bat-shit crazy woman. The possibility of getting together with anyone was not going to happen.

Perhaps that was the purpose of my vision; I would not go there but I would learn. With my heart beating I would see. It made me address my relationship with Dan. So I looked at Dan and I from every possible angle. I looked with clarity and without the interference of my ideals of right and wrong. I was breathing now; I did not want to stop breathing. I did not want to say goodbye to the joy and happiness now in my heart. I did not want to hurt Dan, but I realized our relationship had become a prison. I was being held inside by walls I made out of guilt and duty. A twisted belief that I was responsible for the happiness of another. I knew this was why I would never leave. Had it not been for that powerful vision of love, I would never have allowed myself to consider my freedom.

May 11th, Dan was in surgery for aneurysms in his left knee. I cursed those damn aneurysms throughout his body; I was scared for him. He had enough surgeries, enough issues, but I was afraid of something else. There was the possibility of amputation, and the thought terrified me. My terror was not just for him, but also for me. How could I be so selfish? How could I worry about me? Was I falling back? I did not want to fall back to that depression; I did not have the strength to carry this. No more God! Please get him through this; please don't ask me to take on anymore. Please don't take anything else away from him. These were all the wrong thoughts. Everything was wrong. I was selfish. This was not how you love someone. I remembered those times Dan told me I didn't love him. He was not being miserable, not creating some self-fulfilling prophecy. He was in fact stating what I did not know to be true: I did not love him. At least I did not love him as I should. I cared, I felt for him. He was and always would be Jodie's father, and my friend. Yet, no amount of history together was going to change the truth.

I saw Dan differently after that. His harsh words, his anger with me, his days of silence, were not him being mean; he was just out of ways to say "please love me." All those times I was trying to calm the anger, to create peace and harmony were futile. I would never have been able to fix things because I did not have it in me. I could not find the love, not the one he needed. I had made our relationship an overwhelming weight of responsibility. There is no love without free will, I could no longer bury the truth.

When is the right time to do something you know is going to hurt someone. Is there ever really a right time? Christmas, birthdays, family birthdays, anniversaries, surgeries, graduations, dance recitals, there is always something that you feel makes it a bad time. The truth was Dan and I were living in a perpetual bad time. We were both depressed, and overwhelmed by illness and financial burdens. The misery was inescapable and instead of building each other up we were tearing each other down.

I spent weeks trying to digest and comprehend all the overwhelming changes in my life: the new emotions, the new air filling my lungs. I will be the first to admit there is much about life I do not know. But the one thing I did know, that I believed

I knew for sure, was who I was. I thought nothing could ever take that away from me. Yet here I was, completely dazed and confused. I had spent a lifetime searching for truth, and thought I was almost there. Now I realized I knew nothing. I did not even know myself. The shock of realizing that the only thing I thought I knew for sure was an illusion, was an all encompassing and surreal experience.

Like Moses in the Ten Commandments, I was walking, looking for answers, looking for truth. I knew I was going to end my relationship with Dan; I knew I had no choice. What I needed clarity on were the reasons. I had to make sure there were no outside influences, and that deep down in my heart, my core, my soul, my very being I could find no other option. I could feel the pull of the universe telling me to do this, I knew that this was the time. Either I did this now or I would never do it. The day I made the decision was the day the weight of the world left my shoulders. I was not leaving because Dan was terrible, but because I was so incredibly unhappy, unfulfilled, empty and hopeless. I had lost sight of me.

On May 31st, I told Dan that although I might be confused, I did not think I could stay in the relationship any longer. Around June 6, I gave him back his ring. I was so sad, sick and ashamed that I could not make it work. That I could not fix it. That I hurt another person like this, especially that I hurt Dan like this. Yet at the same time, I would not back down, for it was the most important decision I had ever made in my life. As my mother used to quote, "To thine own self be true." The adage had never meant so much to me, as it did at this time in my life. I had been living a lie. Even to myself I had been lying. The truth had finally set me free.

Chapter 12

Forgiveness

And as I carried the weight of my anger,
I convinced myself I could do it for eternity.
Ignore the pain and misery,
I would not put it down till I won.

What a magnificent victory that would be,
if they one day said they were wrong.
For then I would finally be free,
I could unload the weight of my anger.
And there stood my ego laughing,
so strong and self assured.
While I rode the winds of redemption,
it darkened the light in my soul.

Had I not listened to that ego voice,
there would be no need for my control.
I would have seen I had a choice,
I could unload the weight of my anger.

I started walking around May 1. At first two kilometres was a chore, but by the end of June I was walking five kilometres a day and had lost 17 pounds. People would tell me I was glowing, that I had changed, that I looked different. I was glowing, but I was never going to tell anyone why. How could I when I could not even believe or comprehend it myself? I gave up bread, pasta, potatoes and rice. I ate salads, salmon and chicken. Food was no longer controlling me; I was no longer looking for answers in the fridge, I was finding them walking and looking in the clouds, or at the horizon above the lake. Walking became my church. I felt like I had been blessed. I know that is an odd choice of wording, but it is the closest I can think of to try to explain the incredible change within me. I stopped watching TV, although I had never watched it much. Most importantly, I stopped reading newspapers and political blogs. Anything that might make me angry or sad was simply removed from my routine, and replaced by only positive energy.

By September I was walking 7-8 kilometres a day. I would go out for 90 minutes, every day or night. Listening to music and cherishing my reward of 15 minutes sitting by the lake. I was getting in touch with my true spirit, with my faith. It had been years since I had reflected so deeply on life. I had totally lost touch with who I was, with the heart and soul that brought me here. I was taken off my blood pressure medication and started sleeping better. I had lost 32 pounds, a number I never could have imagined. What's more, the process seemed effortless. Like the weight on my body, the burdens on my soul were disappearing; I was learning to live again from deep within my core.

I was in love. Nothing helps in the will power department, more than having a vision of love. It was just that though, it was a vision. I spent a year using it to help me heal. I never knew its source, or whether my vision was a test, my lifeline or my future. At times I thought maybe it was a connection from another life. I had no explanation for how I could feel what I was feeling. There was nothing in my history, nothing in my logical mind that could explain it. Maybe it was God or my mother getting my attention from heaven, sending me something, so far outside the realm of possibility to me, that I had to notice it? Regardless, I felt love at the age of 50; it brought me back from the brink. This love turned an angry earth woman who felt like she was 70, back into a happy grateful woman. One who needed to be reminded she was not 27.

Writing this has not been easy. There have been moments of doubt. Should I be doing this? Is what I am writing of any interest? Do I look like a fool? Yet I proceed, I have kept going and I realize that it has been years since I was so engaged in work. I am well aware that the process of writing this may be as important as finishing it. I can already feel the difference. I am building again, creating, challenging myself. My fingers are dancing on a keyboard, not for an audience, but for me. Everything in this book is about taking personal inventory. I could say if it helps one person then it is worth it, but I already know it has, for it has helped me.

I am healing. I would like to say I have healed, but I am afraid, afraid of going back, afraid of losing this passion. I feel different now, more so than at any other stage in my life. I am amazed at how I have changed, not just on the surface, but inside. I am open to these changes, I am not fighting them – I want to feel them. I want to immerse myself in whatever fills my cup and gives me pleasure. I know my core principles. I am not overly worried that I will follow some dangerous path to hell, but those chains I let bind me – those irrational puritan thoughts – I am reconstructing, rewiring, rebuilding.

My sister tells me she is seeing a part of me she has never seen before. It is not just the old me coming back, but a new me, like a part of me had been trapped inside for most of my life. Friends keep telling me how happy they are to have me back; they notice this instantly. They also tell me I have changed. I am surprised and humbled by all this. I soak it in, not for the attention, but to try to grasp the lesson, to try to find the answers, to try to explain an intervention without sounding crazy.

For the first time in my life, I want to dance; I mean really dance. I never liked to dance, and now I can't stop dancing. I feel foolish but I do not care. The freedom from all of the things I let own me is a new form of intoxication. The hope and happiness that comes from being in control, knowing my destiny is in my hands. I have the right to self-determination and I am practising it. I will never again be a slave to anger, to victimhood. Or is it more? Is it the power of faith and is it my reunion with my basic instincts, love, hope, faith and freedom.

I am not born again. My relationship with my faith, with God, has always existed. My faith has always been a very personal thing, I never discussed it with anyone. I cannot imagine who else I would talk to when making moral decisions, when looking for the right way, the right path, the right choices. I may love and respect my fellow man, but he is just as weak and imperfect as me. Man's rules are for maintaining a civil society and do not always reflect what is right. I have tried to see a life where there is no God. I see many foundations of our society already crumbling, in this new somewhat Godless world. So on what do we make our stand? Is it our parents? A connection to the earth? A science of which our knowledge changes with each generation?

What has changed in my life? None of the circumstances that brought me to depression are any different today. Events still happened, and I am still struggling with some huge issues. So why the difference?

How does one single moment in time erase that much pain and helplessness? How does one moment so drastically change a life? For all of my endless search for truth, if there was one thing I thought I knew for sure, it was me. Yet in that one moment in time, I discovered I did not even know myself.

The gratitude that swept over me opened my eyes and my heart. Gratitude had so sorely been missing. I could not see it for I was stuck in victimhood, lost in helplessness. Yet the events of the gala brought me to that incredible moment of gratefulness, not implied, not platitudes, but true, heartfelt gratitude.

The face of love and the feelings, the passion and the breath of life it inspired, to this day remain a mystery to me. I cannot believe that this was something buried in my subconscious. I can only see it as a means to turn my life around. It was those feelings, that desire that made me want to live, it helped me to see joy. Happiness and joy were something I could not find, I could not imagine. No amount of money or event – nothing existed inside me that brought any feelings of happiness. Yet now here I was instantly awakened, breathing, feeling, desiring life and wanting to know love.

I needed to have been open, to see it. I would never have let the image inside me, had it not been so unfathomable as to make me laugh and say "really"? Had it been any other image I would not have seen it. I would have dismissed it just as I do with anything that does not fit, or is not right, but not this. It was just too incomprehensible to ignore. So I let it in. I looked, I thought. I entertained the concept, and let it wash over me. I had not been alive for so long that the feelings of joy overpowered my thoughts of right and wrong. I gave in to the moment instead of banishing the thoughts. I let myself be weak and human.

I could see now; everything became clear. How long had I been looking? Yet it was always right in front of me. I had lost control of me. I had become a slave to my burdens and my troubles. Instead of shedding the weight on my shoulders, I kept piling it on and thinking I was fixing things. I was not. I was picking up problems and sapping my energy. I was trying to carry a load on my own that I was incapable of handling. My ego was driving the bus. It was only when I saw that the most important thing to fix was me, when I saw what was hurting me the most, that's when I finally shed the hopelessness.

I could no longer live my life for everyone else, I could not tuck away and hide my most basic instincts; I am a survivor. I am strong and compassionate, but I am also human. There comes a point when we all have to ask "Who is my contract with?" I finally realized it was time to live for me again. I had made my contract: Society's expectations. I was living the life I thought the world expected me to. I get responsibility. I love no one more than my daughter. I expect and accept being depended upon by a child, but not the rest of the world. I could no longer listen to all of the things I was doing wrong, or juggle all of the requests and expectations, even those I piled on myself. The moment I let go, as soon as I imagined being free, was the moment I came back to life.

So I set out to fix myself; it seemed so easy. The image of love inspired me and the move towards freedom beckoned me. Armed with faith and gratitude, I started walking. My mind and heart were open; I was shedding anger. I was listening, I was breathing, and I was content in believing I was headed on the right path.

I tried to decipher where I had been, and figure out what brought me to depression and misery. I didn't think in terms of "poor me." I hate to think I felt that way. I know I was wailing at the world; I know people were pitying me, but I was not looking for pity. I was not wanting that. My anger and frustration were against the system, or at least how I saw it. I did not want sympathy, I wanted justice and restitution. I wanted to fix what was broken and gain control of the situation. I wanted my life back! I was helpless and hopeless. I had done everything I was supposed to, and yet nothing went my way. I was angry! The world was not the place I had always believed it to be. I had thought truth, honesty and integrity meant something, but Sam and his lawyer defied those ideals. Right from the start I had already lost, because there is no justice in our legal system. It is only a game that makes the lawyers rich and the law an ass.

I could not control the bully. Why did they lead me to believe that I could? Why do schools insist on believing they can prevent the actions of bullies, that they can control the thoughts of others without giving our children the most basic of human needs, the right to self determination. Zero tolerance makes the child a victim twice. The way to happiness is the control we hold over our own lives, the freedom of thought. Help them find the strength of their own convictions, the inner strength of building their awesome futures. I so wish I could teach that, to teach all of our children to find strength inside themselves, not in the opinion and judgement of others. Raise your children to be joyful and happy, to be secure and strong within their own hearts. Sticks and stones will break my bones but words will never hurt me. Say it, say it over and over and believe it because the only way those words will hurt is if you teach your children to allow it. Yes, someone said something not so nice, and yes it hurt now let it go, their opinion holds no value unless you give it value, do not become a victim.

I know now what brought me to depression: The same environment we have created for so many children. When a child is bullied, and we remove their right to defend themselves, we are removing their right to self determination. I do not care how much you hate fighting. When you take away someone's right to defend, to face their tormentor, to stand up for themselves, you are creating the environment that fosters depression and helplessness. When we tell the child that we as adults will take care of it, and then do nothing except have meetings, we are creating feelings of helplessness. We are saying we will make it better but we don't. We just talk and tell everyone how they should get along, how they should live their lives. We ignore the basic human instinct of needing to control our own destiny. We just take away their rights and do nothing. Is it any wonder these young minds look at the world and feel helpless?

Without a spiritual component being taught, be that God or the universe. Some type of faith to help lift the weight without judgment. To envelope in love those who feel unloved. Why do we think healing with drugs is more acceptable than healing with faith? Just think about the message we are sending to children. No you cannot defend yourself, yes you are a victim, you have been hurt, let's talk about your hurt, let's talk about this ugly world, let's talk about cruel bullies. The world is ugly, let's hide you from the ugliness. What an insane message we spread. Instead of telling them you can choose your destiny, we tell them someone else does. Instead of they can't hurt you, we tell them they can and they have hurt you. Instead of filling their minds and the halls of academia with "life is awesome!", "life is filled with possibilities!", we have a dozen clubs focusing on victimhood. We wave flags showing our victim colours. Honouring that which hurts us.

The reality is, we can not remove their pain in this way. They need to have an outlet that is their own, the biggest right they have is the right to controlling their own lives. That control comes from within. The strength of the spirit within and a connection to something far more powerful, wise, knowing and loving than ourselves. That big elephant in the room that no one wants to acknowledge. I do not care if you want to teach them the name is God, or the universe. Why do we not discuss or consider that depression and anxiety and suicide has increased as our spirituality has decreased? That is how it was for me through our legal system. I believed in the laws of this country, and that our courts were right and just. I believed I would have my day in court to confront my bully, but all I got was legal debt, lies and insight into a system full of corruption. I was left helpless and hopeless; I did not get justice, the system did not save me, I did not get restitution. I got only debt and the most devastating feeling of disappointment. The bully won. They said they would help me but the bully won – not because he was right – but, because they would not let me fight him. No day in court. No moment of truth… It was not the event, not the brutal back stabbing that I endured, the broken trust. That was not what broke me, they hurt but they did not break me. It was removing my right to self-determination, it was tying my hands and making me watch, telling me what I had to do knowing full well the end game held no satisfaction for me.

The goal was for my anger to subside, for the experience to wear me down, for me to give up.

Finally, four and a half years later I did let it go. It was part of my healing, part of my awakening. I did not however do it for the reasons the lawyers wanted me to. No, under Man's rules I would have kept going until I had nothing left, it was in my nature. No one was going to get away with bullying me, no one was the boss of me.

No, it was a powerful moment of truth. The lawyers had sent me a letter inquiring whether I was going to have someone represent me at Sam's bankruptcy hearing, or if I was going to go myself. They wanted to know what dates I preferred? It was the closest I was going to get to having my day in court. I was going to get to face him, to watch him try to lie his way out of it, in front of a judge. He was going to have to stand up and be a man, instead of hiding behind his lawyers and parents.

I read the letter from the lawyers and moved it to the back of my mind. The new me, the one who was alive and breathing, wanted to make sure I did the right thing. I wanted to make sure my judgement was not clouded by anger, that my thoughts were clear and true. I let the letter wait and asked God for guidance. I needed to know what the final lesson was meant to be. Why was it necessary for me to endure over four years of this battle?

It was a Sunday, I was in my office trying to catch up on paper work. The lawyers had sent a second request wanting to know what dates I was available for the hearing. I knew I had to answer, but I was not ready. While I was doing invoices, something reminded me of a friend's father's memorial I had attended the week prior. It was at the Legion. I did not know anyone, but I knew I should be there. Heather had lost her father to cancer. His battle started about a year after my mother's death. We had many conversations, at the dance studio, about how much we loved our parents, what strong forces they were in our lives. We discussed the pain of losing a parent to cancer and the importance of being there for them, to make sure there were no regrets. Heather and I have a connection. There is something in our makeup, our lives, our journeys that is similar. We do not need to talk about little things. I think it is just that we are both aware of the depth of the human spirit, and have spent time searching for the truth.

Heather did everything right over the course of her father's last few months. As I watched her go through the pain of saying her final good byes to her father, I kept my inner torment in check. There was no moment in time that I wanted to take back as much, as the last few days of my mother's life. Nothing in life had ever brought me to my knees begging for salvation like my mother's last breath. It was a lesson in human weakness. I believed it was a failure I would never recover from; it was the day I gave up on me.

So to the Legion I went, on that mid-summer day. I was quite late in arriving. I don't know why. I think I changed clothes 20 times. I had nothing appropriate to wear, I knew I should not worry about a room full of strangers. How I looked did not matter. What mattered was being there for Heather. I walked in as they were finishing off a slide show. The room was full of people I related to instantly. I felt like I had just journeyed back in time to a family picnic in Northern Ontario, or was it an AA meeting with my Dad when I was a teenager in Montreal? I don't know why I felt that bond, perhaps it was just the Legion atmosphere but I felt at ease with these people. I could have been talking to my own aunts and uncles, it was a feeling of warmth.

Heather reminds me a bit of my mother: classy, head held high and for some reason I use the word proper. Not in an aristocratic type of way, just a sense of perspective. She is a strong and giving person, without pretence or pettiness. When I visited the table of her father's memories, I could not help but smile at the Harley Davidson sweatshirt. That was not how I imagined Heather's father, it was a contradiction of the image I had of him. I liked it. The sweatshirt gave me a new perspective on the man she had told me about all these months.

It was the reciting of the Lord's prayer that grabbed me. It had been years since I had heard it spoken with such servitude. Not attending church in decades, I did not hear it much, but when I did it was spoken out of habit, without gratitude. Unlike the feeling I was hearing at that moment, the whole room in unison and with purpose. It gave me pause and made me look inward and wonder when I had let go of that prayer. Religion was being removed from society, and yet it was becoming more apparent to me everyday, that my healing was for the most part a reunion with my faith. A faith in a higher power. Something so deeply personal and incredibly powerful. To not be alone anymore. To know I had all this free will, but also a hand to guide me if I could only learn to take it.

So I was thinking the Lord's Prayer when I realized I had to respond to the lawyers. I could not fully comprehend the meaning of: "forgive us our trespasses as we forgive those who trespass against us." So I Googled it. For some reason a different version showed up, "forgive our debtors." Really? So I was supposed to forgive Sam? I thought about it at length, pitting Wendy the logical who dismissed the notion of listening to a prayer, or the coincidence of the "debtor" version showing up on Google, against the spiritual Wendy, who needed direction, healing, closure and peace.

I remembered the hospital room, as my mother took her last breath. There was a terrifying moment of pain, it was awful and it was wrong. There was a social worker offering me condolences, and there was I looking at her in disgust. Who was she to offer what she could not even comprehend? I was a soul in purgatory. I did not need or want another human to tell me it was going to be okay, that I did nothing wrong. I am more than capable of justifying on a human level, everything I did or did not do. But in that moment, in my heart of hearts, more than anything else in the world, I needed salvation! In almost 50 years of living, the power and meaning of that word never entered my mind. Yet I knew at that moment, I needed salvation. Without doubt, without hesitation, that night I was on my knees begging for forgiveness. I had failed my mother, the most important person in my life. In her moment of need, I had left the room thinking there would be another day.

And in my office, as all these thoughts swirled through my mind, I had a profound moment of clarity. I thought of the days and weeks and months that followed my mother's death. How many nights had I been on my knees, asking for help, for forgiveness? I finally realized, why should I be asking this for me, if I am not willing to do it for others? What makes me more worthy?

That was my moment of truth. I was asking forgiveness for me and not seeing I was not alone in the need for salvation, for forgiveness. The four year battle was not a waste: it was not wrong that I stood up to Sam. He had not made a mistake, he had done it on purpose. It was a bad intention, but Sam was not inherently evil. He had made an error in judgement and his ego had betrayed him. Now it was time to let it go, to forgive him and move forward. Victory was not to be found in complete destruction. I was no longer obligated to fight and I had not failed.

With that my enlightenment blossomed! I let go of all of the money owing from other sources. I let go of believing I might some day get paid back. I forgave all of my debtors and embraced my new found freedom. None of those people now had control over me, in spite of a system that breaks people, ruins them and leaves them helpless. Through the grace of God, I found my right to self- determination and my free will. I chose to let it go and with that another weight was lifted from my shoulders. The chains around my heart had been removed. The power of forgiveness, true forgiveness, gave me one of the most important lessons of my life. I stopped looking backwards, stopped living in the past and crying over all that was lost. I looked forward and took flight, stronger and more confident than I had ever been before. The wolf changed back to the eagle.

Chapter 13

The Truth

The acceptance to look in the mirror and say – I am

The courage to set foot outside and say – I will

The hurt of being told – You are not

The faith in knowing – You are

*The healing, the hope, and the joy
discovered by so many,*

Because - You did!

Thank you Paula

I think of Dan often; he was in many ways my best friend. We had a life together, and that is not something you just throw away. Like any couple, we knew more about each other than anyone else in the world: good, bad or otherwise. I never wanted to write about us. I cannot make sense of it, not without using words that either hurt Dan, or hurt me, or more importantly, hurt Jodie.

Over the course of the last eighteen months, there are two things that I have heard often. I have been told that everyone has the right to be happy, and also that no one is responsible for someone else's happiness. Both are true, but neither can heal the wounds nor remove the guilt I carry. Only time will heal.

As a mother, I want my daughter to live a happy life. I will tell her she is not responsible for someone else's happiness. I will tell her it is wrong to live your life, just to make someone else happy. I want her to know she is worthy of true love and happiness.

So no matter what you read in these pages and in this story, understand that I do not mean to cause any hurt. I will paint myself in a darker light, before I write any words of betrayal. If I could skip every page that had to do with Dan, then I would do so. I ask would it be better that I stay broken, that our daughter had a broken mother? I saw light and I started breathing. I know for me there was no other choice. I made a change in my life that I can only hope, pray and have faith, will lead to a better life for all involved. If I must however stand trial in writing this book, then I can only state that in learning to show more kindness to others, I learned I may be kind to myself. If I stand guilty in a human court of law, I still have hope that I will be forgiven in the only court that matters.

As I heal, as I get closer to understanding my weaknesses and imperfections, I also get closer to understanding love. Each day I get better at listening and less concerned with society's expectations. I am comprehending love on a new level, slowly walking towards people and situations that previously made me uncomfortable. I have also discovered something in myself I had never realized before. So awkward did I feel receiving, that I missed out on the needs others had in giving. Gifts and acts of kindness from others made me feel shame and they made me feel incompetent. I would often accept, express a heartfelt thank you, and then quickly retreat. I would lower my head and make sure I felt no joy in receiving. What was this? What was inside me that made receiving so uncomfortable? Did I feel unworthy or did I feel above these things, that I had no need? Why would I want? I was so wrong, so oblivious to giving being a two way street. If I am made whole by giving without attachment, with no expectation of return, why would I deny others the same opportunity to be whole? This is such a big lesson in my learning to love.

As I clean house, both mentally and physically, I find gifts from days past. I hold them now, and am grateful. I never understood or appreciated these items the way I should have. I took the saying "It is better to give than to receive" and turned it into "You must give and not receive." Yes, there is truth to the joy in giving, it is an inherent need. Perhaps I was unable to give love because I was afraid, or did not know how, to receive love.

I have known hate, never embraced it, and always got past it. I did hate that rapist, but time has removed those thoughts from my mind and heart. When I read of terrible acts against children, anything intentional against the innocents, I turn my eyes so I cannot see. I do not even want to hear these stories because the evil is so unsettling. I become so tormented. The pain in my heart so strong, that I am incapable of controlling the anger I feel rising to the surface.

It would be easier if I hated Dan. Then I could dismiss him and not worry about his future. But, I do not hate. With the exception of the paragraph above, I do not know how to hate. I will always care about Dan. I will always worry and I will always dream of the day that he finds immense happiness and joy. I wish him well, not to relieve my guilt, but because it will mean he has found what I have always wanted for him: true gratitude, faith, love and peace.

Her name was Paula Stableford, and at first I was not going to go. I had plans to head out of town to see my sister and her family, and to spend a couple of days in solitude at their little island retreat. I wanted to work on my book and spend time learning to meditate. There was nothing my soul was craving more than this opportunity to escape to the island with no walls, no demands, nothing suffocating me.

My friend Shauna Brown invited me, she was having a group of woman over for their own private readings with a medium. I believe that whatever brings people peace and happiness is never something to mock or laugh at. When people tell me about mysterious unexplained experiences they personally have witnessed, I allow them their beliefs. I trust that what they tell me is true, within the realm of what they perceive to be reality. It is just I never want to be accused of drinking the Kool-Aid. As much as I have faith, I also temper it with skepticism, just enough to prevent anyone from taking advantage and making a fool of me.

Initially I said no, but a week later I changed my mind. If I went at 2pm, I could still be on the road to my sister's by 3 or 4. My change of heart reflected the new Wendy, who promised herself that she would say yes more often: To invitations out, to new experiences, to life in general. So, at the age of 51, I went to meet a medium, to have a taste of a spirit world experience. If nothing else it would make for great conversation with friends.

That morning, while I was packing for my trip, I realized it was my sister's birthday in a few days. Although I had purchased a card, I felt the need to give her a gift. It lay on my dresser, beautiful and oh so very special: an 18 karat gold bracelet, finely etched and stunning. It had belonged to our grandmother Maria MacPhee. She had received it as a gift from a well-to-do family whose children she took care of while they travelled. It had been passed down to our mother. My sister and I used to wear it when we played dress-up, always thinking it was costume jewelry and never imagining it was real gold. We had so little, how could our mother own something of value?

Being the oldest girl, Mom had given it to me during one of my visits before she was hospitalized. It was a special memory, and I was so humbled to have been given it. I realized though, when I was thinking of the perfect gift for my sister, that this bracelet meant more to her than it did to me. I only wore it sparingly, and when I did, I thought of how my sister would love it. She has very little attachment to material things, but this bracelet held a special place in her heart. I held it and thought yes, as much as it means to me, this is the right thing to do. I then realized I had told Jodie that it would be hers one day; it stopped me. I could not give it to Cherin if I had promised it to Jodie, so I put it back down and decided I needed to think about it.

It was arranged that since I needed to get on the road, I would be the first one to meet with Paula. When it was time I told my hostess I was scared, half jokingly and half seriously. After all, I had no idea what went on at one of these events. I sat down in the room, nervous and oblivious to my surroundings. Paula had heard me and reassured me there was nothing to fear. She did not talk about bad things. I had not even thought of that. I was just nervous in general. I had spent most of my life pretty sure this was all a game, and now I was second guessing myself as to why I was there. I was way too logical to fall for this.

She started off with a big one: "Your mother passed on in the last three years." Did I really hear her correctly, did she really say my mother? Not someone close to you, not someone generic, no she said my mother. "Yes I replied. It will be three years next week." Paula said Mom was with us. She then said it was cancer although she was thinking breast. I said no. She mentioned my grandmother, my Mom's mother was there; she had breast cancer. As she spoke, Paula was moving her hand around her stomach. All I could think of was my Mom's distended stomach. Then she said it: My Mom's death involved cancer of the bowel. Wow! Bingo! My grandmother had breast cancer and my Mom had sarcoma that originated in the bowels. The doctors had thought it was there, bowel cancer or maybe ovarian. It was all a little hard for me to take, and the session had just started. She continued passing along messages that made me cry. She pinpointed things that were eating away at me, that I was having so much trouble forgiving myself for. Here were these messages, so deeply personal that no one else could have known about them. And some of her questions blew me away!

She started to introduce more people. Paula mentioned she saw a man heavily decorated in the war, his name was James. Okay, now I am beyond words. My grandfather, James Rae, was heavily decorated. She then mentioned my father was still alive and saw "RR." His name is Robert Rae, coincidence?

Paula talked quickly as the room grew fuller. She jumped from one deceased relative to another, but mostly it was my mother she spoke of. I got a little confused when she started discussing a girl named Anne, off to the side. Since we had been talking about my brother and sister, all I could think about was I do not have another sibling. Paula is sure I knew Anne or of her. She gets a little frustrated and added the name Margaret or Marguerite. Writing the name down on a piece of paper, she looked up and said it would come to me. So certain is Paula, she knows she is not wrong so it must be me that is confused.

I am now getting used to living on faith, but when it presented itself like this I was completely unnerved. Paula is kind, her spirit is good. My instincts told me this. I was focusing, I did not want to miss or forget anything. It didn't take long for my guard to come down. I stopped worrying about being tricked, my mind and heart opened. I wanted whatever peace, truth or love I could gain from this experience, I could not ignore the gratitude that was filling my soul as she spoke.

Paula established that I had a brother and a sister. She explains that my Mom was always with us, and always loved all three of us the same. Her son was her son: the apple of her eye. Nevertheless she loved all three of us equally. I knew all this. It was in my book. At the same time, Paula said that my Mom worried that I did not know. She was sorry or sad that I did not always share with her how I was feeling. She then said my Mom liked the words I had written about her. I assumed she was talking about the poem I read at her celebration of life. It came out that I was writing a book. Paula brought up drugs and alcohol, which certainly were part of my book.

She explained again that Mom was always around me, maybe she said us. Most often she came as a butterfly or a bird. Instantly I said, she comes as a butterfly for my sister. Paula nodded knowingly and said "Yes, on her shoulder," patting her own shoulder as she told me. I sit in amazement! Not too long after my Mom's death, Cherin told me about a walk she took. A monarch butterfly landed on her shoulder. She knew it was Mom, and chatted with that butterfly for quite some time. It had moved to her finger and she walked home with that butterfly. It had stayed with her long enough to show it to her children. Cherin has butterfly ornaments throughout her garden, in honour of Mom. She knew, she has always known that Mom was with her.

Paula then looked at me and said, "For you she comes as a bird: a – a robin." As if to listen, she hesitated before saying robin. "She flies at you, at your head." Paula stretched her neck and head towards me as she spoke. I knew instantly. The day became even more surreal. While doing yard work the weekend prior, I heard a bird squawking as I was cleaning around the cedars. It was a robin. I looked around the area to see if there was a nest, and there was one. I started talking to the robin, apologizing for being near it. I picked up my rake and headed towards the garage, the robin flew into the garage and then back out, right at my head.

Paula continued "You have your mother's ring but you don't always wear it, you take it on and off. How come?" She was correct, I had a special ring of my mother's. My sister had it enlarged so I could wear it, but now I have lost weight in my fingers and am afraid of losing it. I tell her this. "Uh huh," she says. "But you have something else of your mother's. It is round." "The bracelet" I blurted out. "You need to do right by it" she says, "you need to do the right thing" "My sister" I whisper, "but Jodie" ... and I do not finish my thought. She says " It does not matter to her, she will not care, you need to do the right thing."

I was overwhelmed and excited, I could not wait to present the bracelet to my sister, I could not believe what was happening. I was filled with gratitude. I felt blessed, like I should be on my knees or something. It was beyond anything I had ever thought I would encounter in this life, in this world.

"Who was cremated," she asks. "Was it your mother? Why have you not dealt with the ashes?" She says it does not matter where they go, just do it together. Plant a flower in the yard as a remembrance if I am worried about not being able to visit her, she would like that, perhaps a lily of the valley.....And once again I am speechless. I had been so worried about how Mom would feel about her ashes being laid in Montreal. It was the final piece of my healing from her death that I needed closure on. In a brief session with this stranger I was skeptical of. My mother's love and understanding, her forgiveness, was given to me. I finally found the internal peace I had been seeking.

Jodie was going to be staying with her father while I was away for a couple of days. She was in her room being a teenager while I was doing my last minute packing. I had the bracelet and was looking for a box to put it in, trying to find the words on how to approach this with Jodie. "You know Jodie", I said, "Aunty Cherin has been so good to us, she has helped us out, helped me out so much over the past few years … And with it being her birthday on Thursday I want to do something extra special for her." I continued on and I knew I was coming across very anxious and emotional. "I know I had mentioned this bracelet of Nana's would be yours one day, but I think it would be the perfect gift for Aunt Cherin. I know it would mean so much to her. I feel like I should give it to her." Jodie looks at me like I have two heads. "Sure Mom," she says. "You're okay with that" I ask? "What is the big deal and why are you acting so weird?" I tried to explain but stopped myself, it was all a bit much for me. I needed to digest what was going on in my head before I tried explaining it to Jodie, not sure my daughter needs to see her mother half baked.

So Paula was right, it did not matter to her. Jodie had some butterfly broaches my Mom had given her, they had no monetary value but Mom had given them to her personally when she was younger, those were what mattered to Jodie….I had forgotten about the butterflies. Why had I never grasped the association, my child had, she knew more than me where her Nana was.

The drive to see my sister was a long one, five hours instead of four, but it did not matter, I had more than enough to think about and keep my mind occupied. Five hours to rationalize, to step away from the experience with Paula and see where I had been tricked. What did I say, what information did I give, what did I produce to allow these things to come out?

But I could not. I could not find a logical explanation, I could not analyze my way back to normalcy. I tried. As much as I so badly wanted to believe what happened was real, I had to put the logical side of my mind to work and tear down the facade layer by layer and piece by piece. No one was going to get the best of me, make a fool of me. And so went the typical battle inside my head, spiritual Wendy vs logical Wendy. I had asked my friend before I left what information Paula had about us, all she told her was there would be seven women, no names, no information whatsoever.

I thought about the girl, Anne off to the side. I now knew who Anne was and I was so sad I did not see it then. I was so focused on thinking Paula was talking about a sibling that I could not see the obvious. Anne was my step-grandmother whom I knew better than my biological one. Anne lived to be one hundred and two and I often talk about her, a remarkable woman, an amazing woman whom I did love dearly. The off to the side made perfect sense, she was not blood. My Mom's mother was there and I know how much my Mom loved and respected Anne, but she would have been off to the side, lovingly so I am sure. I would have to ask my sister if the Margaret/ Marguerite means anything to her.

I arrive at my sisters, it is too late to go to the island tonight. I sit down at the kitchen table where they had saved me some dinner. My sister, her husband Mike and their youngest son Steve and daughter Jacqueline are there. I cannot wait to tell Cherin about what just happened, I cannot wait to give her the bracelet, her birthday is four days away but I have to do it now. I love my brother in law Michael, he is solid, he is a great man in every sense, a good father, responsible, humorous, a listener, an advisor. Caring, respectful and the list goes on, I don't live with him so I can call him perfect, the perfect man to marry my sister and raise a family with her.

I hesitate. I have no idea how Michael is going to receive this, I am not sure if I can tell this story in front of Steve and Jackie, but I do, I cannot wait to let it out. I go over everything I can remember, I pull out my papers, the two that Paula had written scrolling notes on. I start to tell the part about Anne, my sister instantly knows it's our step grandmother, I say Paula mentioned Margaret or Marguerite which meant nothing to me, "That was her real name" says Cherin, "when I had called the nursing home to see how she was doing they had said there was no Anne there. We finally determined she was registered under Marguerite, that her given name was not Anne." We looked on the paper that Paula had given me, she had written Marguerite. How could I have influenced that moment with Paula if I did not even know this, if this was news to me. So clear was my memory on this, Paula had sat there, in all certainty looking me in the eye and saying "It will come to you."

I gave Cherin the box with the bracelet and told her the story. We cried, it was so right and so special. As Cherin wiped her tears she said,"I don't know why, you know I do not have attachment to things, but this bracelet means so much to me, it always has". We discussed the butterfly and the robin. I brought up all of the other people, the incredible things Paula knew, the proof that it was them, that they were there.

I then held the second piece of paper, "Paula said that this is for you, that you still had not healed and Mom wants you to read this." On it she had written " You Can Heal Your Life – Louise Hay". Cherin was amazed. Louise Hay was like a hero to her, so much of her spiritual guidance comes from Hay House, from the Chopra Centre. "That book is on my list," she said, but even bigger was the revelation. "You know, I had seen how Mom was helping you and some of her grandchildren, how she was reaching from the other side, but I was waiting for her to help me. Maybe she always was helping me, maybe it was her that led me to the

Chopra Centre, to my yoga and meditation."

I had always thought that I was the black sheep of the family, that I had some connection to nature, to the spirit of the human soul that was different. I saw for the first time that my sister is just as connected, maybe even more so.

The next morning Cherin dropped me off on the island, the weather was cold for June 1 and the old cottage had no heat. I was fine with this. A little warmer would have been nice but I was just so happy to have some time away, some solitude to write. I was supposed to be working on my book but I could not even think about it until I digested the events of the previous day. I spent the afternoon writing down everything Paula had said while it was still fresh in my memory. I did not want to lose this, I had just lived the most incredible half an hour of my life and I needed to keep it close. As I digested it all, worked it through in my mind, I kept coming to the same thought. From this day forward my life has changed forever, not me, not who I am but rather my understanding of the world around me. My faith in a higher power is no longer based on subtle hints, events and coincidences. I have now witnessed that without doubt there is an afterlife.

Paula had touched on many things that afternoon and I could not possibly cover them all and explain their significance with any type of ease. She had mentioned my separation, she asked who had broken the trust. All I could think was that there was no affair, she explained there were other ways of breaking the trust, she said it was not over yet. I could not comprehend what she was saying so I let it go knowing I would have to sleep on it.

It actually took me weeks to realize it was me who broke the trust, by ending the relationship I had broken the trust. I did not like the wording but it was the truth, unless she meant something else. She said he was very smart and brooding, that was Dan, incredibly smart, but with that came an impatience for others. When she said it was not over I just let it roll. I was pretty sure for me it was. Time however has shown that was not what she meant.

Less than two weeks after our meeting Dan came down with an inexplicable ailment that landed him in hospital and has so far left him in pain and unable to walk on his left foot for over two months. His life and journey over the last few years have been so wrought with pain and sorrow. A very smart and strong man has been left incapacitated by aneurysm surgeries meant to save his life. We have no idea if they would have burst, but how does a man walk into hospital feeling fit and healthy see himself two years later cut up all over his body, unable to walk and unable to function without a million pills a day? I wish I could lift him up, I wish I could give him the emotional blessings that have been granted to me. I cannot undo my leaving him, not by going back in time or going back now, it would only result in a combined suffering. I feel for him and I do whatever I can to help, but I cannot own his pain, not the way I used to.

It was during the drive to my sister's that it hit me. At first I thought it was just that I had so much else to think about, once again however, time has proven that was not the case. My spirit guide or my guardian angel had left me, the inexplicable love that had carried me all these months was gone, nothing felt the same.

Paula had told me a few things about my future, they were intriguing, fun, exciting. She had mentioned a man that would fill me with so much joy, but I chose to put it aside. I had not planned on meeting with a fortune teller, I was meeting with a spiritual medium and that is where my interest lay. For some reason hearing about my future seemed like cheating. It may also be that I was not ready to accept so much joy. I was not feeling worthy.

I spent a great deal of time that afternoon at the island thinking of all of the people I was wishing good things for, wishing that they too could experience a moment like I had. There were some people that I knew some time with Paula would probably make a world of difference in their lives, would help them through the incredibly difficult time they were presently living in. I became consumed with this. How could this help this person and that person? My soul was alive, I was seeing life as possibilities, I was seeing that I was on a path with new found wisdom and knowledge.

That evening I walked around the island 20 laps to get some exercise and to try and stay warm. I was starting to feel a little cold but there was no way I was not going to spend the night in the place I had waited so long to be at. I made a nice salad for dinner and wrote a letter of encouragement to someone I really cared about. My book had still not been touched. I opened all of the battery operated candles my sister had purchased and placed them throughout the cottage, I then grabbed some real ones and prepared them for night fall. When darkness came I sat by candlelight and counted my blessings, all of the pressures and the burdens of the outside world were washed away. I felt no fear alone on this island and I focused on letting go of all of my fears about the future. I would not worry about where Wizbot would be in the months to come. I would not worry about how I would survive when I was 70. I would focus on staying healthy and capable enough to work. I would not worry about what Jodie chose to do with her life, as long as she was happy. I would not worry about Dan and how he was going to get by, I would help him but without the worry. I was focusing on letting go of all my future fears and just living in the moment, just breathing in the beauty of this life.

In the middle of the cottage, surrounded by candlelight I spoke with all of the relatives that said hello to me from the spirit world. I spoke out loud as there was not a living soul around. I let my spirit out, I let it dance, I removed all of my human resistance to the mysterious and unexplained, my social proprieties were pushed aside. It was a celebration of life, of the intervention that had saved my life, that had brought me promise and hope. It had gone, it had left me, I could have been so sad but I knew it was time. I was on my own now, that which was holding me up, helping me through was now letting me fly on my own, I was almost healed, it was time to go forward without additional aide.

It sounds ridiculous, it sounds insane but it was remarkable. For 13 months I had been guided by an external force. A love from another dimension so pure and powerful. Everything had seemed almost effortless or will power was in abundance. I had started the age of 50 in misery and walked into 51 a new woman. I think it was my mother, she was brilliant. She used the most bizarre method, the most amazing plan to make me see.

I had been granted my salvation.

Chapter 14

Sanctuary

And the soul said this is who I am,
while the ego said this is who you could be
and the brain said don't be silly.
So the soul thought she should be someone else.

And the soul said this is what I need,
while the ego said you could have more
and the brain said it's not logical.
So the soul thought she was not worthy.

And the soul said I am hurting,
while the ego said you are invincible
and the brain said you are no longer capable.
So the soul found life to be painful

And the soul said I am dying
while the ego said you never were much good
and the brain said we're running out of time.
So the soul found what it was like to live in fear.

So the soul banished the ego and hushed the brain.
And there in quiet meditation and prayer,
She discovered the truth of who she was.
The boss of the ego and the brain.

The soul said this is who I am,
And she found joy in the freedom of being .

The story of Anne was one of the most enlightening gifts I ever received. It was unexpected and one that grew more important as time marched on. It was in 2007 when Mom, Cherin and I had flown to Nova Scotia to visit Anne. Anne's last remaining sister had fallen and broken her hip at the age of 94. During our drive taking Anne to visit her sister in hospital she told us the story of marrying our grandfather, Alfred.

Anne grew up in Cape Breton as one of five sisters of Lebanese descent. Their family owned the general store in Mulgrave, supplying almost everything to the local community. In fact, during wartime, I believe they even sold caskets. When her father passed, Anne ended up running the store. Her sisters had married and moved on. For whatever reason, Anne never married. She was a beautiful, kind hearted, gentle woman deeply rooted in her Catholic faith. She was completely committed to the church, living a life of divine providence.

My Mom's mother, my grandmother was a fiercely independent woman in her day. Maria Evans, born in Newfoundland in around 1917, had a car and a job at the age of 17. Very uncommon for a woman in those days. My grandfather was her second husband, her first one dying of illness very early on in their marriage. Maria or "Rye" as everyone called her, had succumbed to cancer in her fifties. It was on a Sunday that she died. Remarkably she had informed my Mom a few days prior, that Sunday, was going to be a beautiful day. How did she know?

After Maria passed, Alf had gone to Cape Breton to look up Anne and asked her to marry him. And so her words to us on the drive to see her sister were this. "I married your grandfather when I was sixty and we went on to have 28 glorious years together."

Anne's simple words were one of the most powerful life messages I had ever received. Love can come at any time, we never know what great happiness is in store for us. And we never know from sadness what joy may follow. Keep your heart open and always have faith.

—∽—

It was not the first time it had happened during the intervention however this time it was the most pronounced. It was December 2014, months before I had met with Paula. I was getting ready to head to the airport with Jodie and my nieces: Avalon and Alanna. We were going to meet Cherin and her family for Christmas dinner before they headed out on the trip of a lifetime. Their whole family was going to spend Christmas in Australia, and they were staying overnight in Toronto to make an early flight the next day.

I was brushing my hair and the reflection startled me. It was my mother. I couldn't put my finger on what detail, not the eyes, the cheeks or the nose. It was nothing in particular, yet so clearly I saw her. I was used to seeing my father, not always happy about it, but I definitely carry his DNA. This was different. It was perhaps the third time in the last few months I had seen a resemblance, something I had never seen until this year. But this time it was shocking.

We were at the restaurant, my sister, her husband Michael and six of Mom's eight grandchildren. Out of the blue my sister stopped talking, looked at me and said, "Wendy, you look like Mom!" Cherin was as surprised as me. Neither of us have any of Mom's features, yet that night I "looked like Mom."

It was just a fun thing, an odd occurrence, perhaps the weight loss and exercise, who knows? We talked about it a few times that night. Then I never gave it a second thought, until today, as I write this. As I become more in tune with my sixth sense, my instincts and the clues around us, I wonder. I cannot help but wonder if that was Mom, visiting, wanting to sit and enjoy dinner with her grandchildren. Insane, perhaps. Yet I can't say I have seen that reflection since that day. It's been almost a year and I am the same weight and hair colour; however, since that December day, I have not looked in the mirror and thought, "I see Mom."

Upon reflection, after a year of writing and 18 months living this new life, what have I learned? What is the lesson? My intervention and Paula. What was this all about and why did it happen to me? Is this insanity? Did I drink the Kool-Aid or was I given a gift ? I cannot go back, I know that, nor do I want to. Once your eyes have been opened and your soul so warmly embraced, you see and feel everything with a new perspective. This new vision is an exciting motivator. It's like seeing the world through the eyes of a child again. Everything is so new, fresh and full of possibilities. What could be more amazing then living life filled with possibilities?

My vision of love, the soul that entered my heart for all those months, who made me question everything I knew about myself. She, who inspired me to walk all those miles and lose all this weight. Today her purpose, the meaning became clear. In writing this story, in reliving my life and seeing on paper everything that shaped me, the answer came: She was Me. She was the side of me that I buried, that I feared, that I ignored. By leaving my heart open all these months, by believing an answer would come, today I saw. There is no doubt that I loved her during that time, but her purpose, aside from giving me hope, was so I could see the beauty

I had shut out of my life. Yes, at 51 the little girl had emerged. She came out into the light and danced, after hiding backstage, for so long. She had been frozen by her fears: to step out into the open, to be seen, to be acknowledged, to love and be loved.

I have come out of the closet – the spiritual closet. I still don't know where I fit, I just know I no longer fear love. All men are not rapists and being a woman is not a weakness. I don't think I am gay, but I no longer run from that which I do not comprehend. I no longer care. I want to face it. I want to face life on every level and live without fear. My first step was learning to hold someone's hand. To break through the coat of armour we all wear to save us from judgement. To walk in faith is to know courage and grace. To live outside of society's opinion is to know freedom. To see love in everyone is to find the light inside your soul, where there is love there is no darkness.

Our walks through despair are but moments in time. When we can understand they are shaping us for ourselves, not for others. "They are happening for us, not to us." (Thank you Paula.) We are then free to go through them without fear. We can come to accept the lesson from a position of faith, not victimhood. Allowing ourselves to be a victim is different than the act against us. The act took place, we were wronged, we were hurt. Once we have acknowledged it, we must be cautious not to let it own us. It is our free will that affords us the ability to change our view and control our hearts. To face forward in hope, not backwards in helplessness.

I walk down this new road. It is so much more beautiful than any I have seen before. How did I get on this path? What brought me here? Everything is different and I am in awe. How is it possible to have lived such a wonderful life, and then after a storm, discover the best was yet to come. To have found a level of joy that a broken spirit could not have conceived, could never have fathomed.

The focus, I no longer rely on my eyes alone to see. I have discovered the mind, body and soul are capable of viewing life through a lens that is a multitude of times more powerful. The clarity, the intensity of the vision. We do ourselves no service by limiting our thoughts to a standard protocol. Reality does not end at our fingertips. We have so much more to learn and to explore. We have locked ourselves in a cell, guarded by society's expectations. When do we remember that we used to know how to be free.

It may be normal and safe, but is it right? Is it healthy to accept our lesser selves? Do we just live life following the herd? I can no longer live like that, I find no happiness there. I seek and I desire more. The thought of leaving this world without fulfilling a purpose. Unfulfilled potential, afraid to speak, afraid to love. Love that ignites more love can burn for eternity, ignored it dies unkindled, left smothered by fear.

I stopped fighting it. I thought life was a test strewn with hurdles and road blocks. I believed each barrier I broke down, got over or under, was meant for me to prove I was worthy. I was wrong. It never was a test of my strength; it was a test of my faith. I was invited to listen to the voice inside me. The path of love and joy flows, it is the spirit within you that knows the way. My sister had told me that, that it is supposed to flow. Yet again Cherin knew the way, I just needed to listen. Or, as seems to be the way with my life, I needed to live it to understand it.

I sit here smiling. In these moments of solitude I discover my deepest needs. I block out the noise of the world around me, and in the silence and meditation, I hear what beats true in my heart. My vulnerability allows me to encounter this moment of passion, and recognize my need for unity within, to become whole, to feel complete. Is this it? Is this the end result of my search for truth? What are the elements of life that I require to be whole?

I received my salvation through Paula, my mysterious medium friend. I did not even realize it at the time. When I said I felt blessed and thought that was odd, it makes sense to me now. The words she shared could only have come from my mother. It was her forgiveness and understanding I needed. No other person on earth could have granted me that. No one else could have released me from my overwhelming suffering of guilt. I had never expected I would have found my salvation in this lifetime.

I clearly see how faith has provided me with inner peace, happiness and life. How magically throughout my life, when the need was greatest, my call was answered. I can no longer deny the truths I have lived. Life is about understanding free will, and understanding that we all have a soul to feed. We are unique and beautiful spirits, each one of us arriving on this earth in perfect innocence. It is about allowing you, about living life under your own contract. Don't let the thoughts and blinders of others rule you. Don't let anyone be the boss of you!

Life is abundant, joyous and magnificent. Or it is ugly, heart-breaking and painful. We rule our thoughts. At the centre is our core, our energy and light that lives for truth, to dance free. It is there; it exists. It moves freely, joyfully and without shame in the faces and actions of children. It is why we are so drawn to and protective of them. We see our true spirits, our true selves as we were born, as we were meant to be in the innocence of children. When we explore the happiness of children, it is not stature, possessions or the opinion of others that brings them joy. It is energy, what they create, what they learn.

Can it be that there is yet another dimension to our existence that needs to be seriously explored? That spiritual healing may be the most important facet of next years modern medicine? That the Bible, although a true work of wonder and wisdom, is but one piece in the puzzle of human evolution? Are we capable of evolving to another dimension? When we try to expand our understanding of the freedom and light that comes from faith, will we align ourselves with new truths?

To keep an open mind, I thought I had one. Yet while I was telling myself I accept that someone else may think that way, I was still dismissing it as an option for me. To peel back layers of social indoctrination does not happen overnight. It takes time and practice to move from theory to belief. I embrace each new day with an open heart and mind. In doing so, moments have greater meaning and truth becomes more tangible.

As long as I allow others their thoughts and never try to control. As long as I don't judge and I learn to accept, then the conversation becomes honest. If I focus on gratitude and giving in every meeting, then I will leave those meetings feeling whole, as I will receive what I have given. I will know love if I give love but I will never know love if I try to keep it. It is free and abundant but can only be found if it is shared. It cannot be caged, hoarded or smothered. It must fly free and then it will expand.

I am not certain of my final destination; I just know that I am back to loving the voyage. I found my rose coloured glasses and I do not want to lose them again. I lived that way in Whitby, I lived that way when I was a little girl lying on the ice staring at the universe. Those were the times when I was living in harmony with my soul. I found comfort and happiness in my gratitude, and faith in something higher. I was not fearful of tomorrow, not angry and not burdened. I was free and in control of me.

I am however one step better today. That "new me" my sister saw, that person who was back but different. I spent so much of my life trying to shun the woman inside me, her weakness and her frailties. Finally I have come to accept and love the softer side of being me, to let that other light shine, not hide in shame. I have stopped listening to the ego that wants to prove, and started listening to the heart that wants to heal and give. It was there, it was always there. The best years of my life were when I lived the needs of my soul. Now however, I am ready to receive as well. No one will bully me. No one will reign over me. Not because I am a warrior, but because I have found the incredible power of love, acceptance and faith.

My claustrophobia is almost gone, that suffocation, that desire to bolt. It is slowly disappearing. I saw it, I saw love and it was not possessive and controlling. I had no idea it existed. I am free, my heart is dancing. I found the music for my soul and I have finally discovered what it feels like to be whole, to be complete, to allow me.

When I left my mother's arms, I believed it was the last time I would ever be held, or ever need to be held. Such a need would be a weakness, a failure, a shortcoming. Such was my understanding of adulthood, from here on in I would be the holder.

I was wrong. When I looked in the mirror and saw my mother's face in my reflection, I now know my mother had been holding me. She was helping me through the most difficult time in my life; even my sister saw it. I was not alone and love lives on, it does not end with the body's last breath. Why me? Why this miracle? Why this gift?

The closest I can come to answering these questions is to say, I was finally willing. I was willing to open my eyes and my heart, to see love as a gift and not a weakness. I was never meant to live in that dark, and ugly world I allowed to grow within me. It was only there so I could see and understand the difference. The world is dark and ugly, if you look for it. But it is brilliant, abundant, and joyful if you seek beauty. Seeking beauty softens the heart, lightness and love, nature and potential. Our own inner abilities to create the world we want to see. We create it, we control our vision, our view of it. We have the power within – our free will – not to control others, but to control our own view. When do we finally understand this lesson? When do we stop thinking the world will be a better place when everyone lives as we think they should? The reality is, if everyone focused on living the lightness of their own soul, we would know heaven on earth.

Gratitude and love. Be grateful, embrace the gifts and happiness of others, find your better self. Don't focus on negatives, focus on what fills your cup, and fill it with only good things. That which hurts and concerns you, put it off to the side and deal with it as you are able and willing to. Do not own it; do not let it poison your new and beautiful cup. Know that you are exactly where you are meant to be right now, see the past as only a lesson and the future as one of possibilities. Make your next step one of which you will be grateful and embrace the power of knowing you have control over you. Fill that cup with beauty and gratitude and it will overflow with abundance. Hope is always in reach. Know that true love is in all of our hearts. When you let your spirit shine through, when you love yourself you will become light. Others will be drawn to it. There is nothing more appealing to a lost ship at sea than the beacon of a lighthouse.

My search for truth is unfolding. It does not end with one final answer but rather continues with incredible lessons. They are eternal. All emotional fear stems from our own pride and ego. We fear society's judgment, yet we know we should not judge. So stop, stop judging and you will free yourself from judgment. We cannot see the beauty in our own souls when we judge our brothers and sisters. As has been taught for eternity, stop worrying about that speck in your brothers eye and you will start to remove the plank in yours. Being honest with ourselves and others is the most freeing and loving way forward. There is no test to fail, just knowledge to gather. Whatever peace, joy and serenity I find I want for everyone. It is a treasure hunt that everyone wins for the bounty is endless.

My past is not my shame, it was my classroom. To progress to the next level I had to learn the lesson. To learn the lesson there were times I had to fall, and from the bottom I learned acceptance. To get back up I changed my thinking. Life is not meant to be lived in fear but rather freedom from fear. You are good enough, you are more than good enough for you are truth, love and healing. This is all the permission you need to be happy. The only person that will ever know or understand your journey is you. You cannot run to the guest room to get away from sleeping with yourself, so you must learn to love yourself. When you learn to love others without judgment you will find the beauty in your soul, it is here that you will know what truth is. It is here that you will learn to love the limitless potential that is you.

On what authority do I write this? On a two million dollar diploma, the one that taught me you can lose all and have more. May 1 2014 I could hardly walk a mile. On June 6 2015 I walked and ran a half marathon: thirteen point one beautiful miles of hope and healing. On September 30th 2014 I put pen to paper in gratitude and I wrote about the intervention. Today, October 7, 2015, I finished writing a book. Two accomplishments impossible to have conceived in both cases thirteen months prior. At the start of 2014 I was lost and broken, I was "dead Wendy." Now, in the final quarter of 2015, I have found my way to true joy and happiness, unaided by pills or professionals.

Life is awesome! I truly have lived a pretty amazing one on intentions and free will. I had the love of a great mother. For all of humanity, I believe the love of a good mother is the gift that will continue giving for generations to come. It is not poor me, I am healing and finding sanctuary. I am guided by light, the lightness of being. I have found the courage and the strength to reach for that limb, the one that taunted and eluded me.

This was my story. No matter how uncomfortable, or frightening, I was compelled to share this. If there is one teenager, alone, fearful and lost who finds inspiration in this. If there is one middle aged woman thinking life has passed her by and she finds renewed hope. If there is anyone who reads this and it triggers a light within their soul. Then my awkward indulgence had purpose.

Who else but a woman who is not afraid of being called bat-shit crazy, would write about a divine intervention? Perhaps that is my purpose, a stubborn and simple woman not afraid to speak her truth.

Sanctuary, that one place that every heart needs to beat freely, without ridicule, without judgment. To be home, to be safe, to be held and to love and be loved.

My journey, my free will, my faith – my sanctuary!

As the song goes:

I once was lost but now I'm found,
Was blind, but now I see.

Amazing. Amazing Grace.